This Book Belongs To

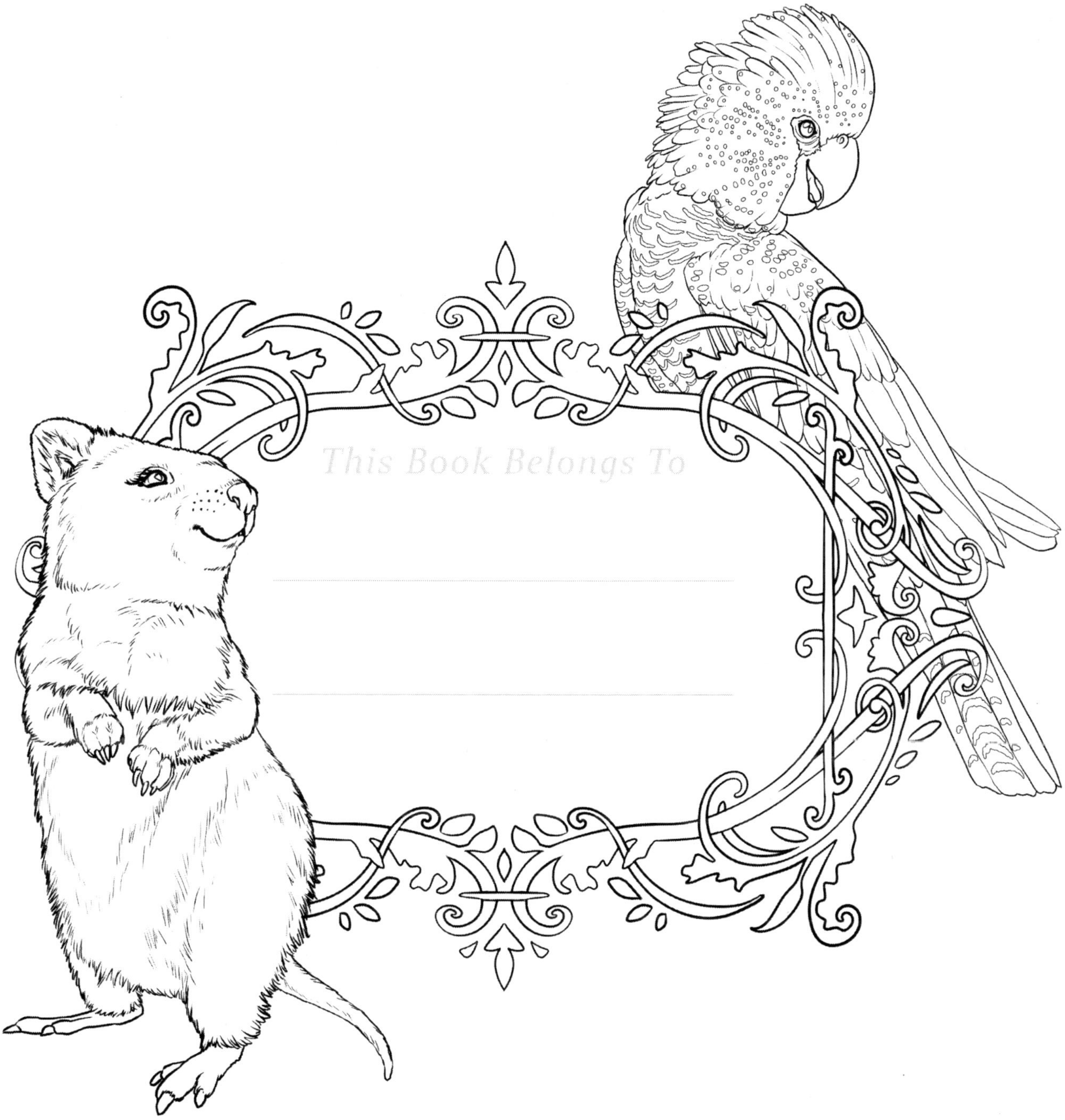

Includes 2 each of 25 Australian animal and wildflower colouring images by Selina Fenech.

As an artist, colour is a thing of magic in my life. Colour creates shapes, forms, and feelings in the artworks I paint. Laying colour onto a blank page is when I feel closest to true magic, when I feel happiest and most relaxed, and it's through what I create that I share my love of magic with the world. Through my colouring books I want to share that same magic with you.

This colouring book is a special one, created with a deep sense of love for Australia after the devastating bushfires of January 2020. More than ever, we must cherish and protect the animals and plants that share this beautiful world with us. Together, we can create a better future, while remembering all we have lost.

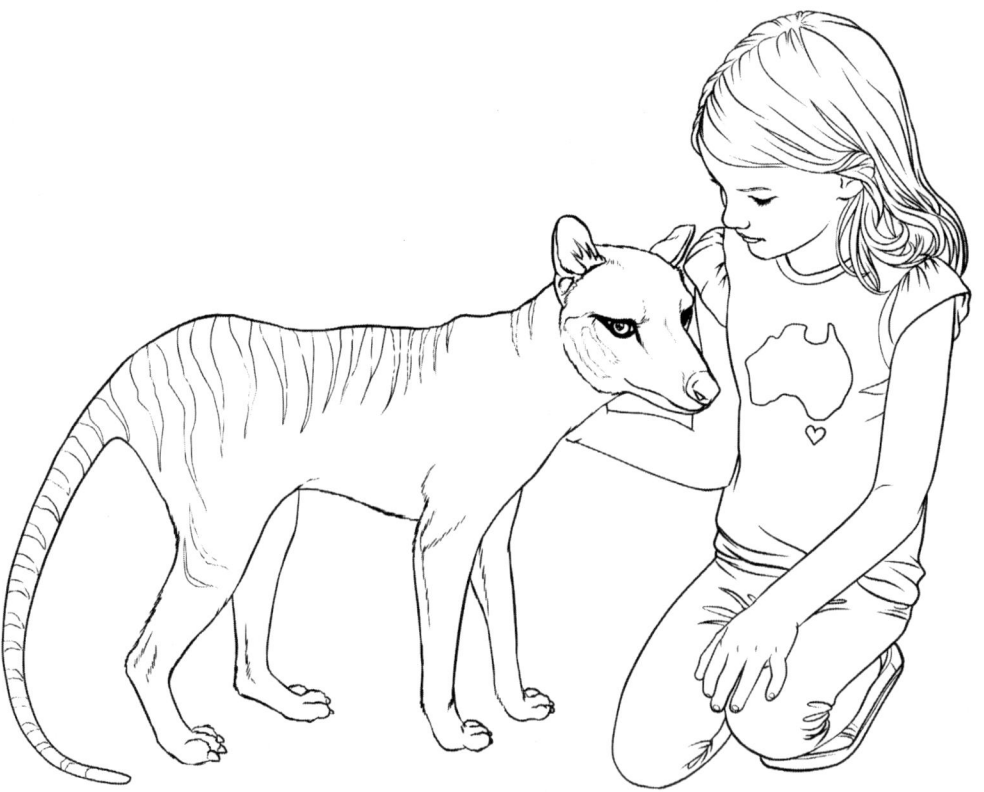

The artist's daughter, who suggested the creation of this book, alongside Australia's most famous extinct animal, the Tasmanian Tiger.

Australian Animals and Wildflowers Colouring Book by Selina Fenech

First Published February 2020
Published by Fairies and Fantasy PTY LTD
ISBN: 978-1-922390-07-3
www.selinafenech.com

Artworks Copyright © 2020 Selina Fenech. All rights reserved.
No part of this book may be reproduced in any form or by any electronic or mechanical means including information storage and retrieval systems, known now or hereafter invented, without permission in writing from the creator. The only exception is by a reviewer, who may share short excerpts in a review.

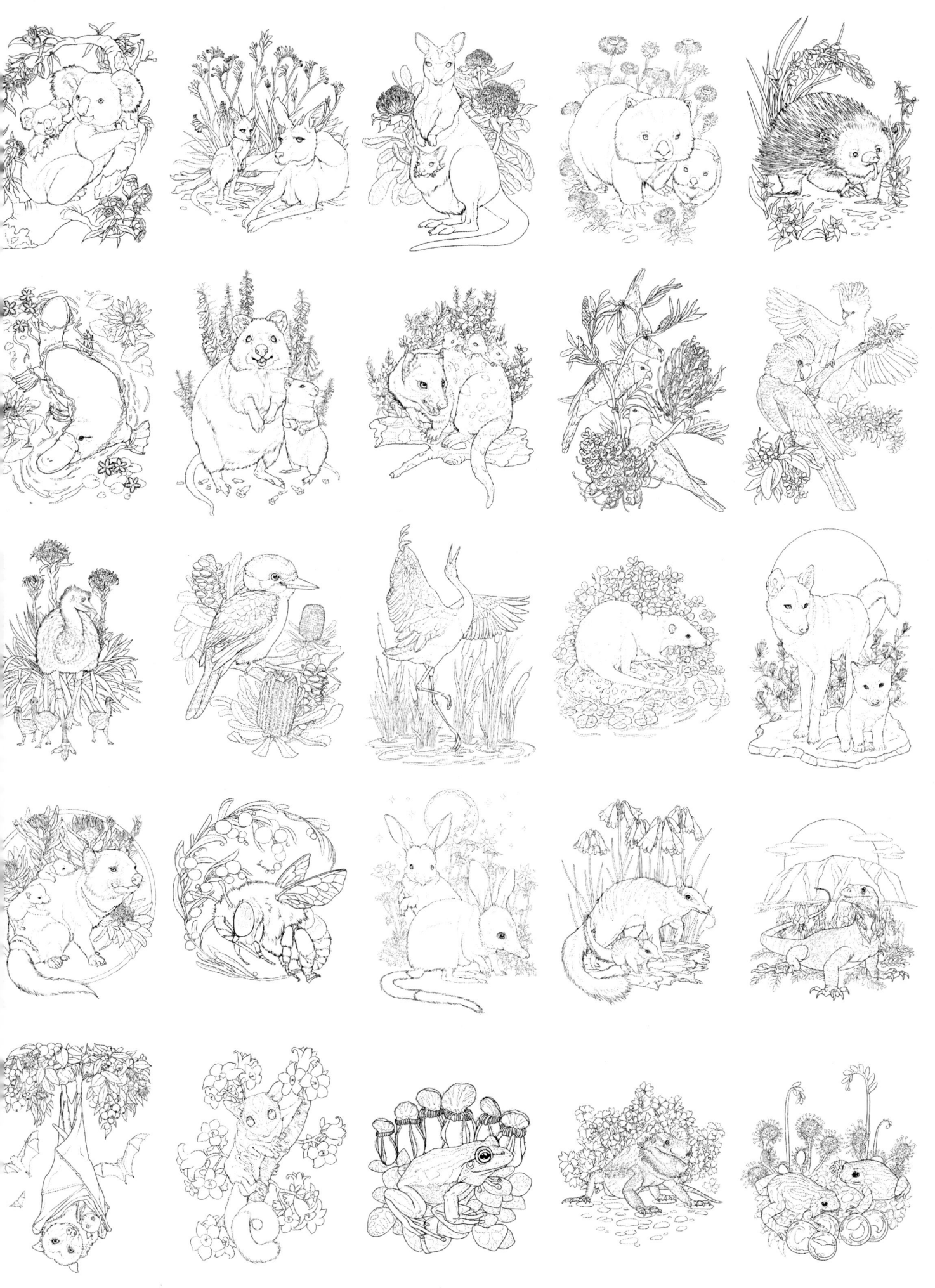

WALLABIES AND WARATAH

Related to kangaroos, but generally smaller, these macropods also carry their joeys in a pouch. Waratah flowers are most famously bright red, but can also be white, pink, or yellow.

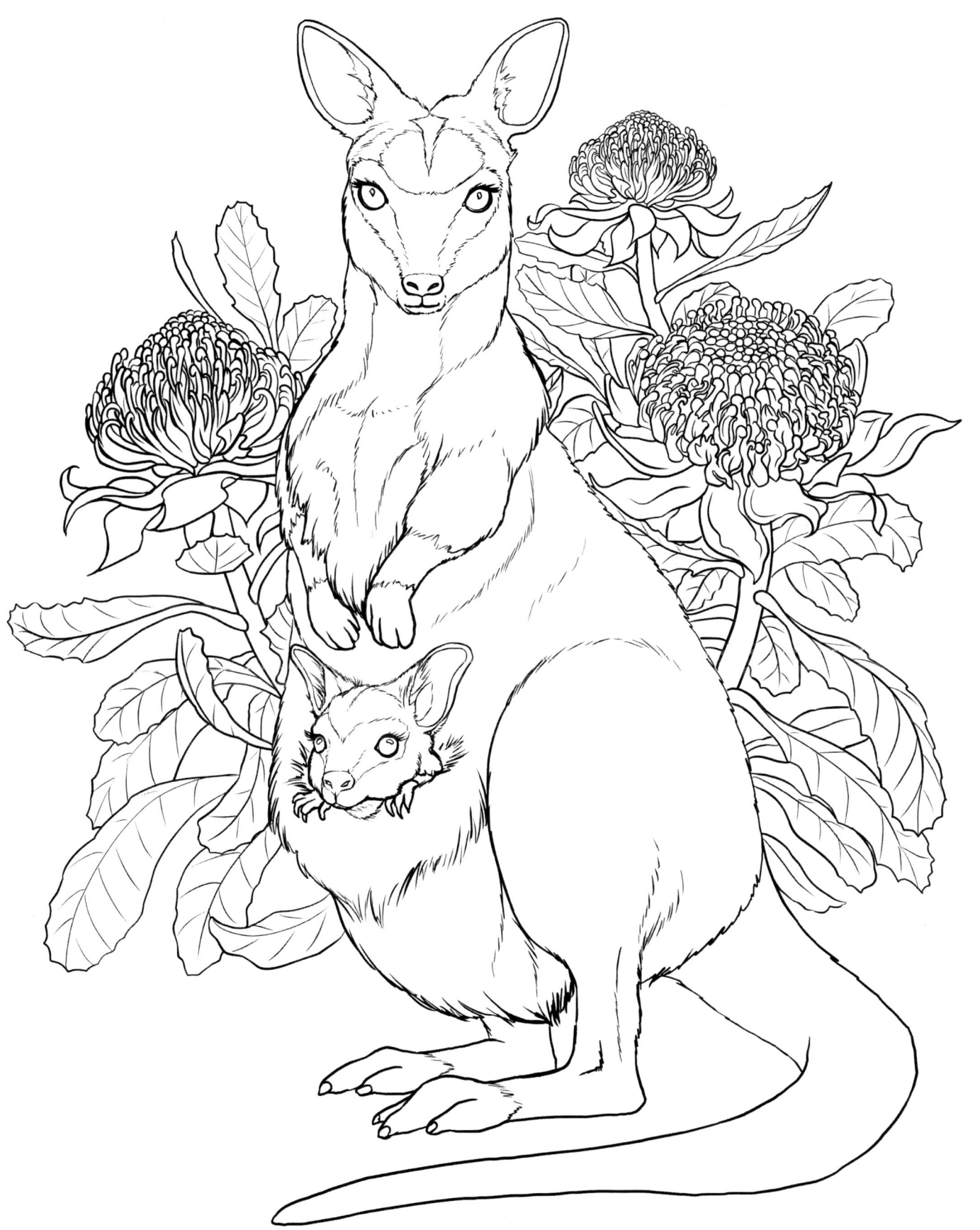

WOMBATS AND STRAWFLOWERS

Wombats, like most marsupials, have pouches, however their pouch faces backwards to avoid filling with dirt while they dig their burrows. Strawflowers are also known as everlasting daisies because their straw-like texture means they make beautiful dried flowers. Commonly yellow, but also appear in a range of pinks and white.

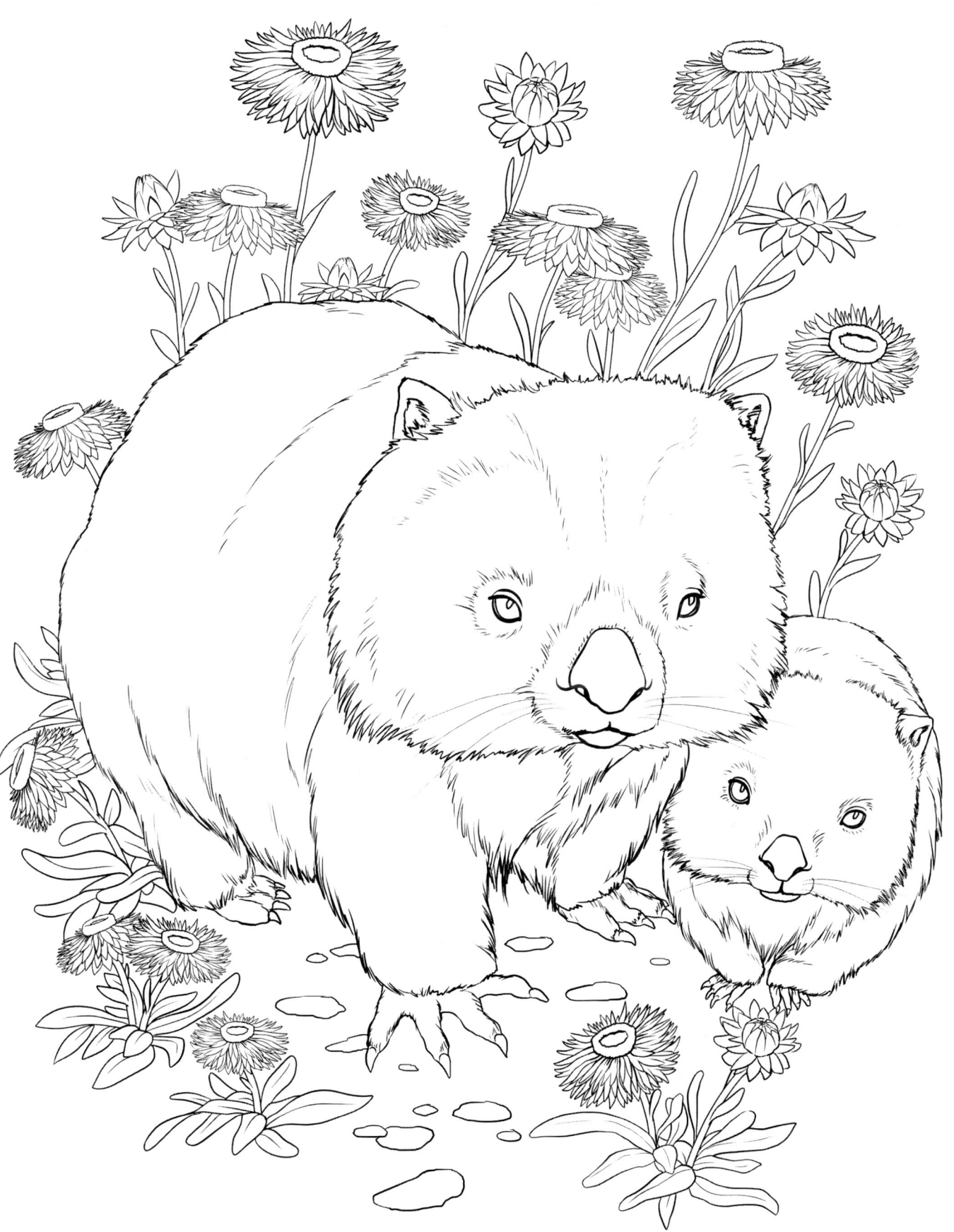

GREY KANGAROOS WITH KANGAROO PAW FLOWER

One of Australia's most iconic animals, known for their hopping motion and for carrying their joeys in a pouch. The Kangaroo Paw flower is named for its flower's resemblance to paws. The flowers come in many striking colours.

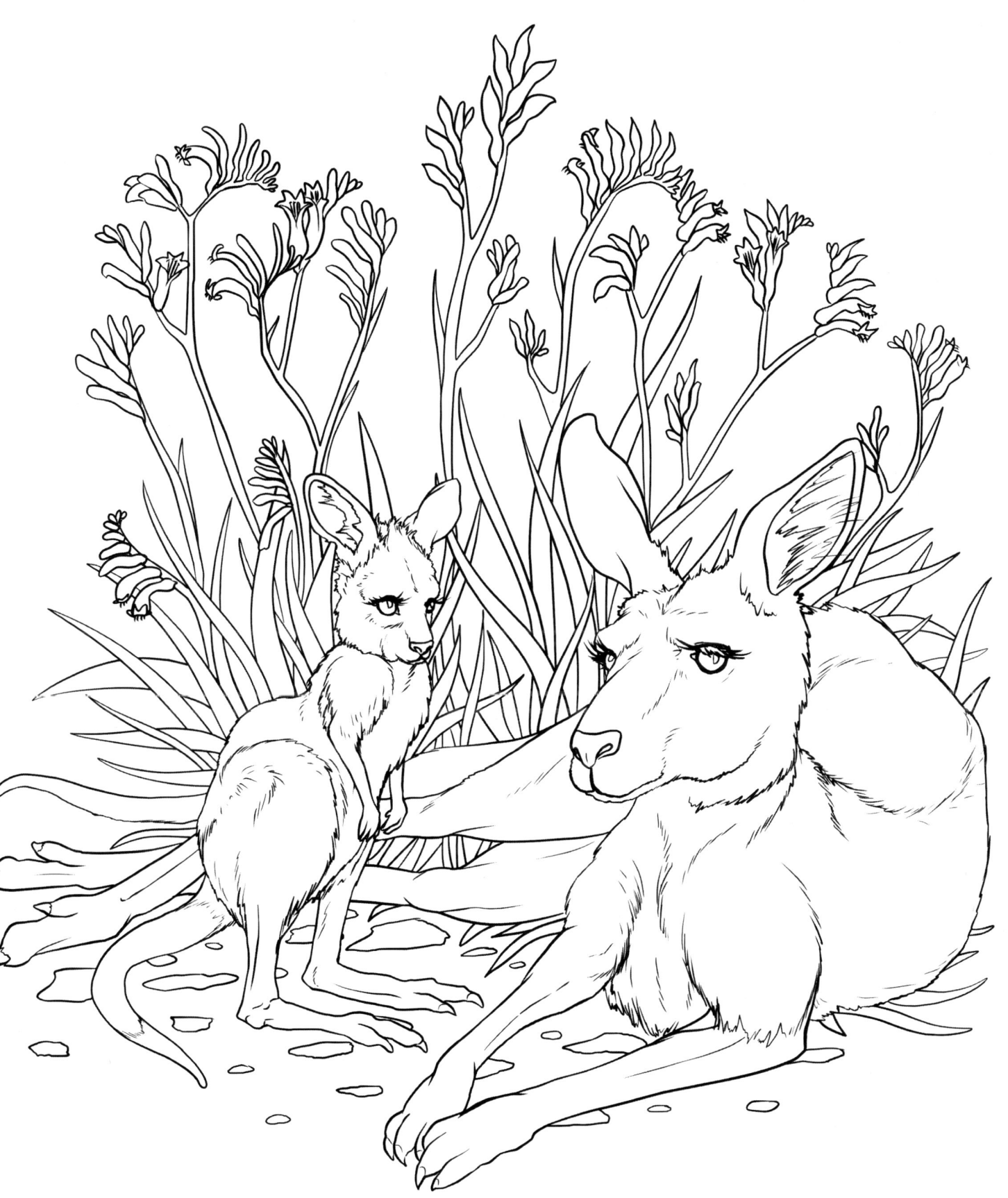

KOALAS AND EUCALYPTUS

Australia's favourite fluffy animal, Koala's feed almost exclusively on eucalyptus leaves, which are toxic to most other animals. Koalas have two opposable thumbs on each hand for better climbing. Eucalyptus (or gum tree) blossoms are commonly white, yellow, pink, or red.

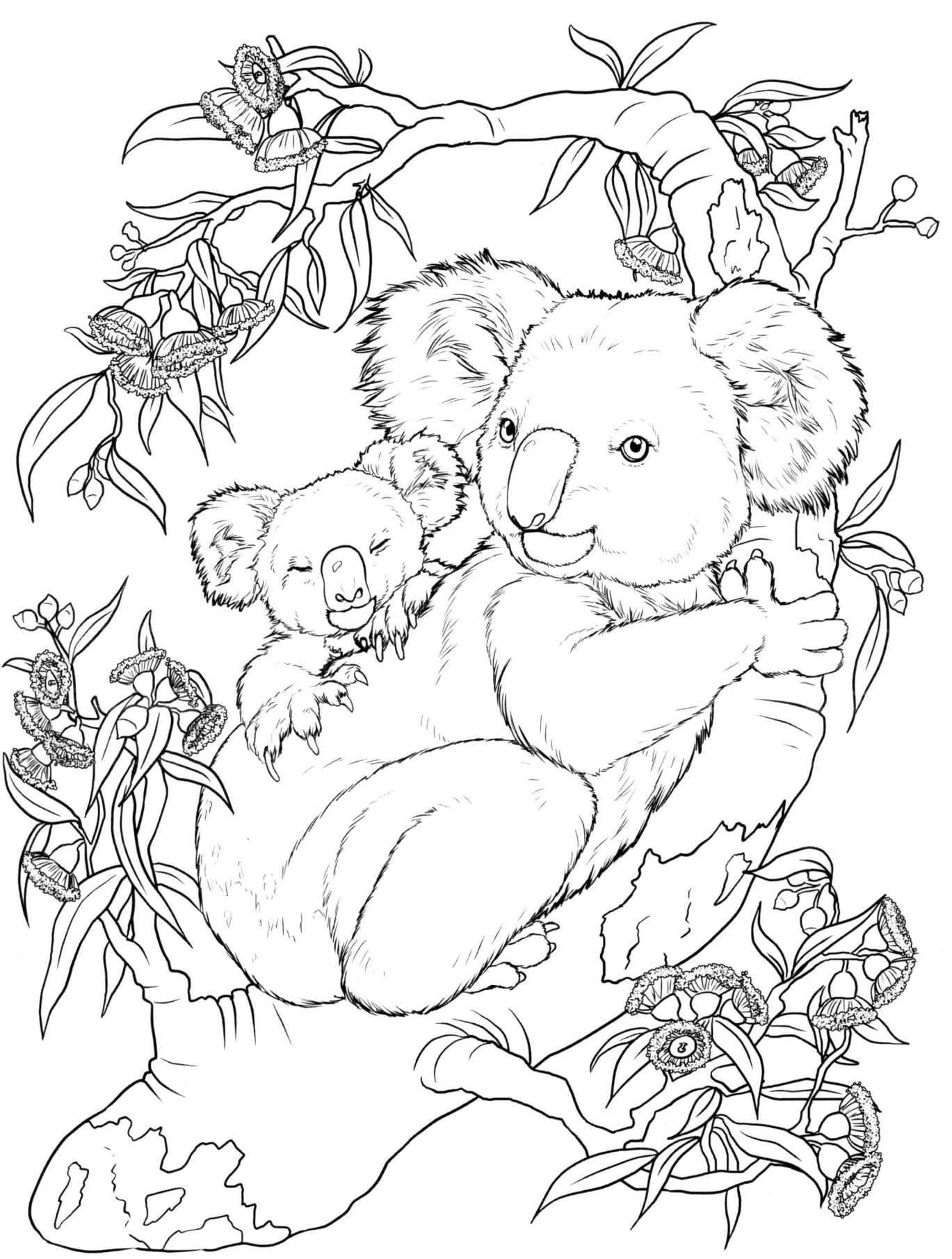

ECHIDNA WITH COWSLIP ORCHID, FLYING DUCK ORCHID, AND SNAKE ORCHID

The bizarre echidna is one of the world's only two monotremes - warm blooded, milk producing animals that lay eggs. They eat ants and insects with their long tongues. Cowslip and snake orchids have yellow flowers, while the flying duck orchid is a deep maroon, and shaped like tiny flying ducks.

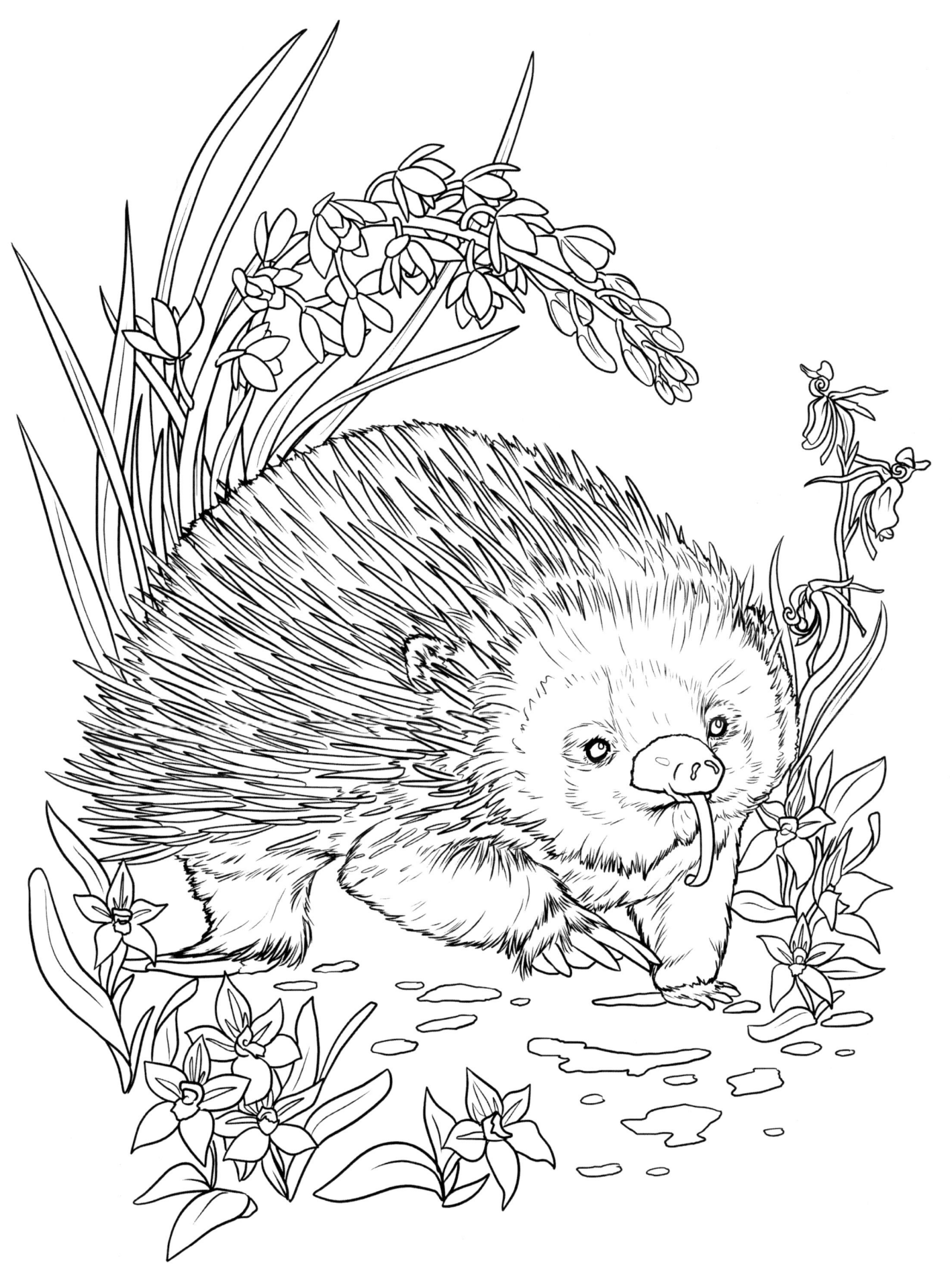

PLATYPUS WITH WATERLILIES AND NYMPHOIDES FRINGE LILY.

One of only two monotremes in the world, the Platypus is an egg laying mammal. With its duck-like bill and webbed feet, early reports of its existence by British colonists were considered to be hoaxes. Fringe lilies flower in white or yellow, while Australian varieties of water lily are generally lilac.

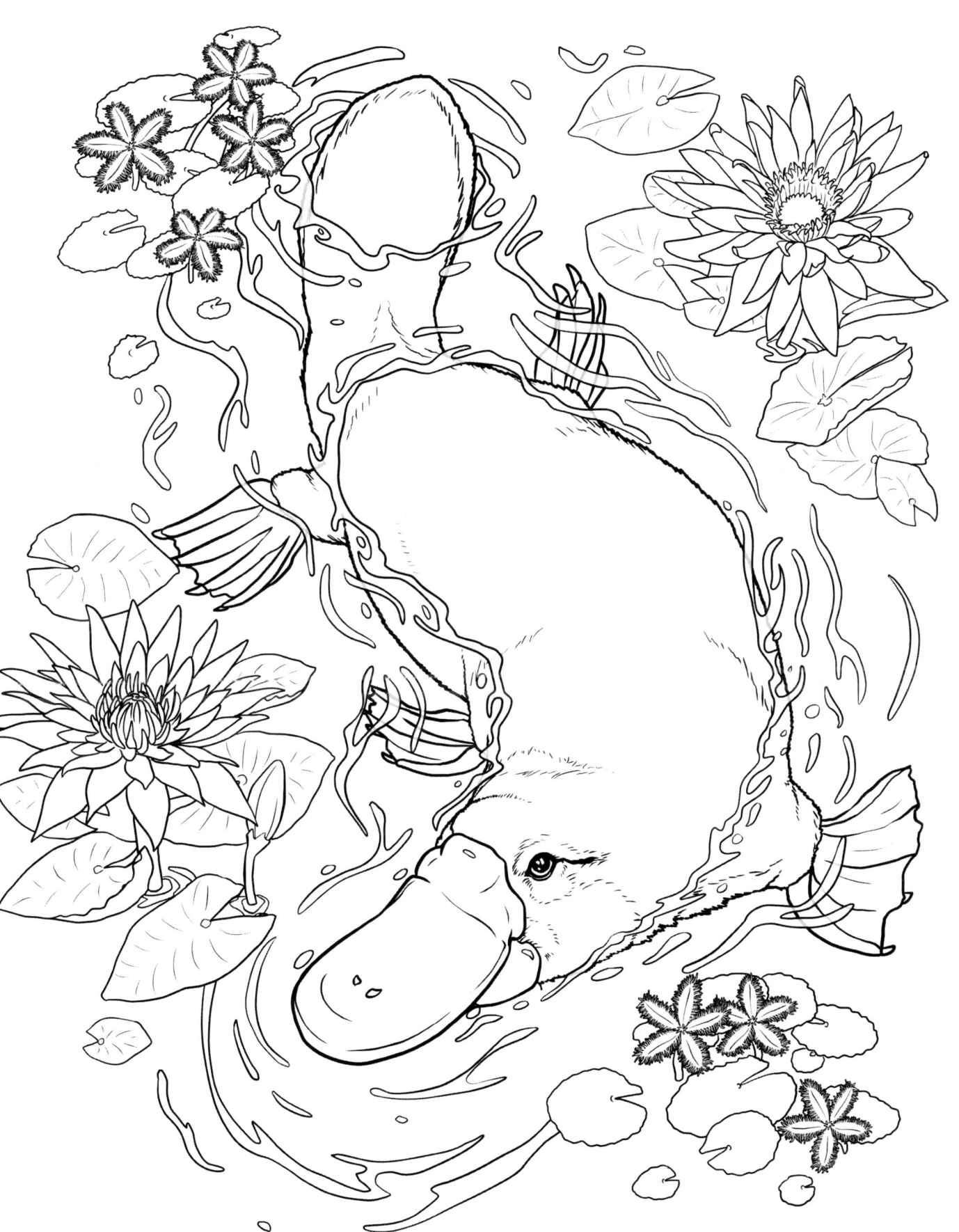

QUOKKAS AND COMMON HEATH

Famous for being Australia's happiest animal, quokkas are part of the macropod family along with kangaroos and wallabies. The common heath is a prickly bush covered in masses of pink, bell-shaped flowers.

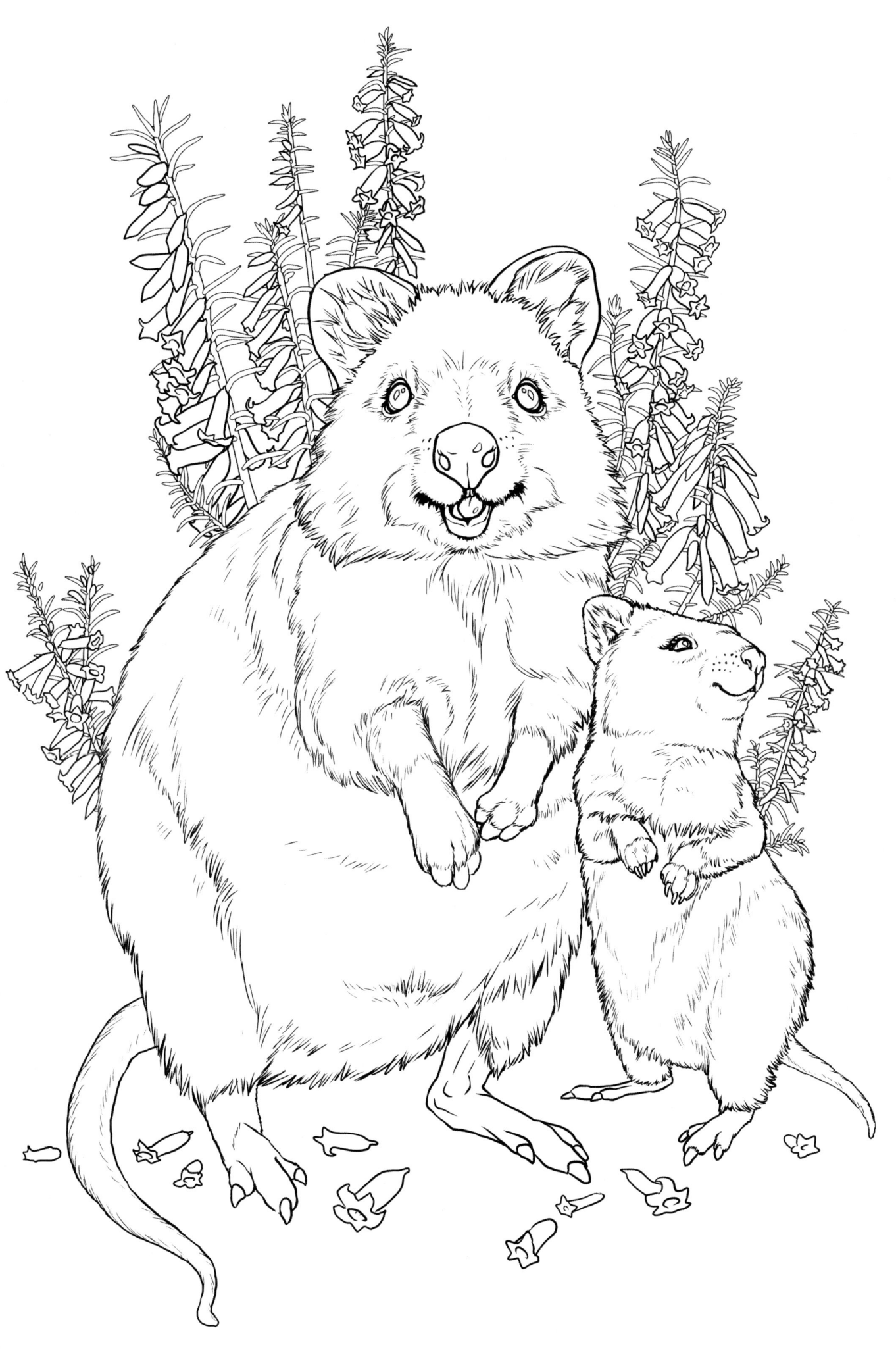

QUOLLS AND CROWEAS

Quolls are a catlike, carnivorous marsupial. Its babies are the size of a grain of rice when born, and will sometimes piggy-back on their mother once they are too large for the pouch. Some quoll species only develop a pouch during breeding season. Crowea's star-like flowers come in violet, pink, or white.

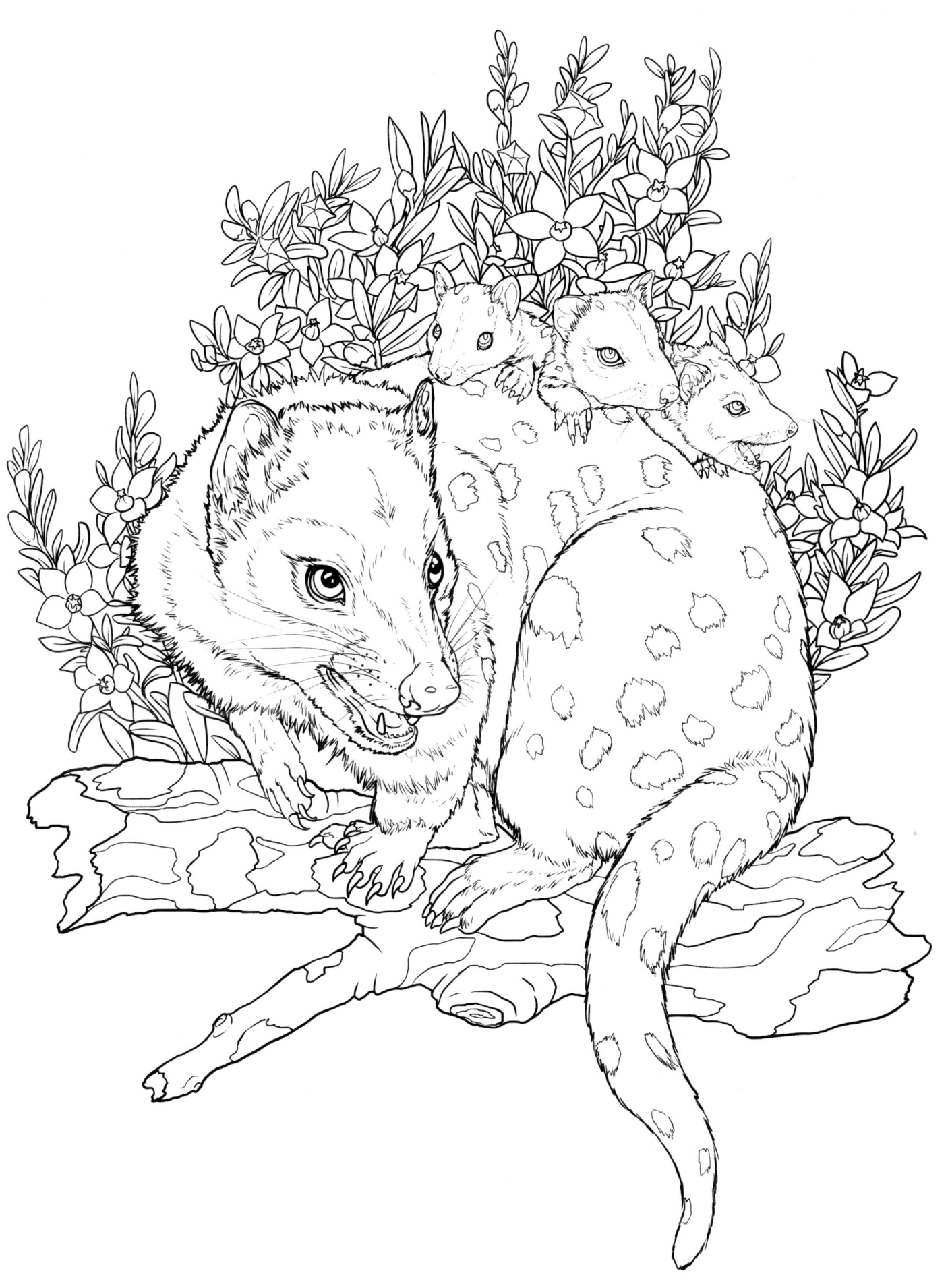

RAINBOW LORIKEETS WITH GREVILLEA

This particularly cheeky, vibrant, rainbow coloured bird feeds on fruits and nectar. Grevilleas come in a multitude of varieties, and (like the lorikeet) in many colours of the rainbow.

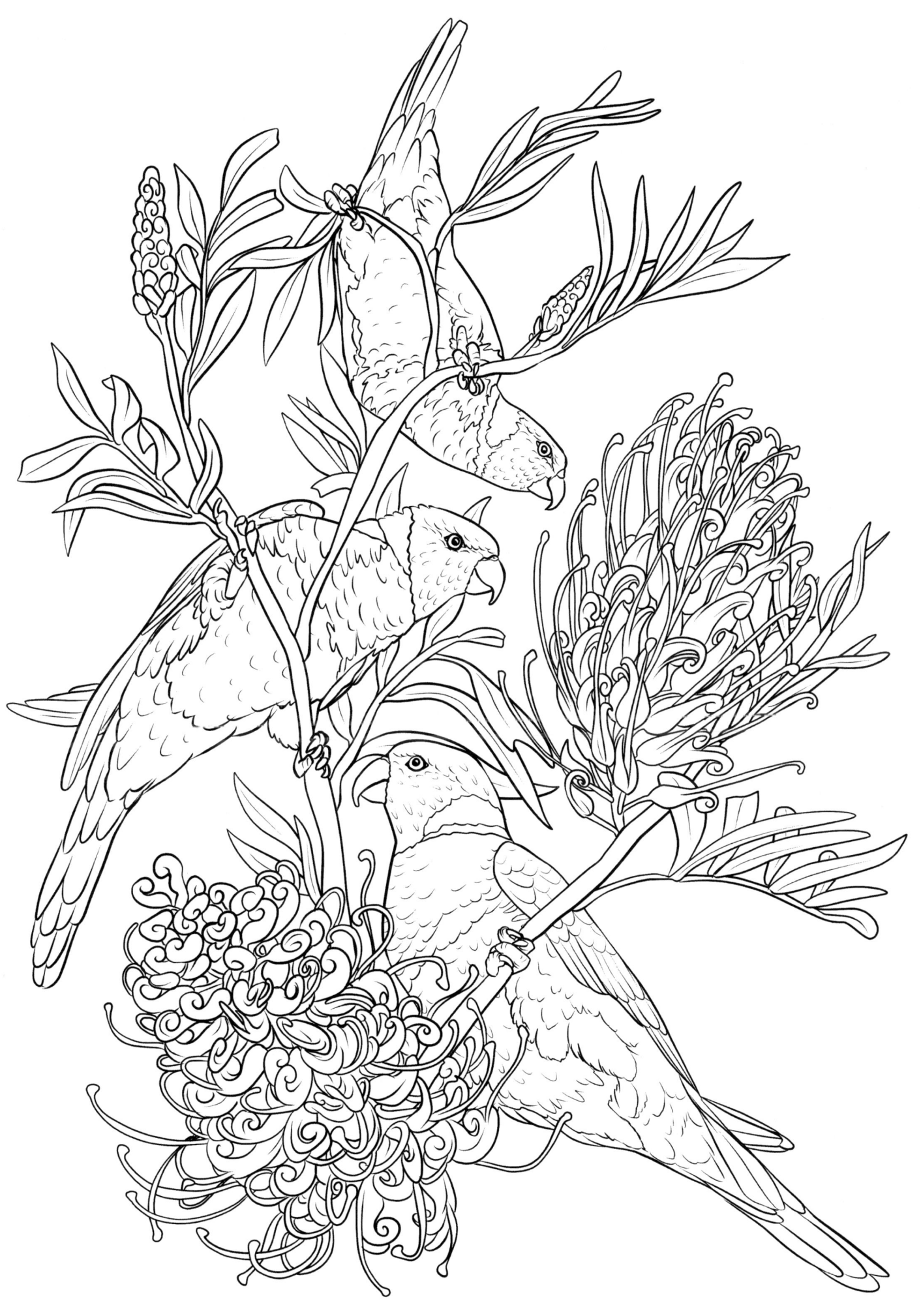

BLUE BANDED BEE WITH WATTLE

Blue banded bees have fluffy orange fur on their thorax, with black and blue stripes on their abdomen. They are solitary, and while they have a sting they aren't agressive. There are many varieties of wattle with flowers of different shapes, but all are similar in their iconic stunning bright yellow.

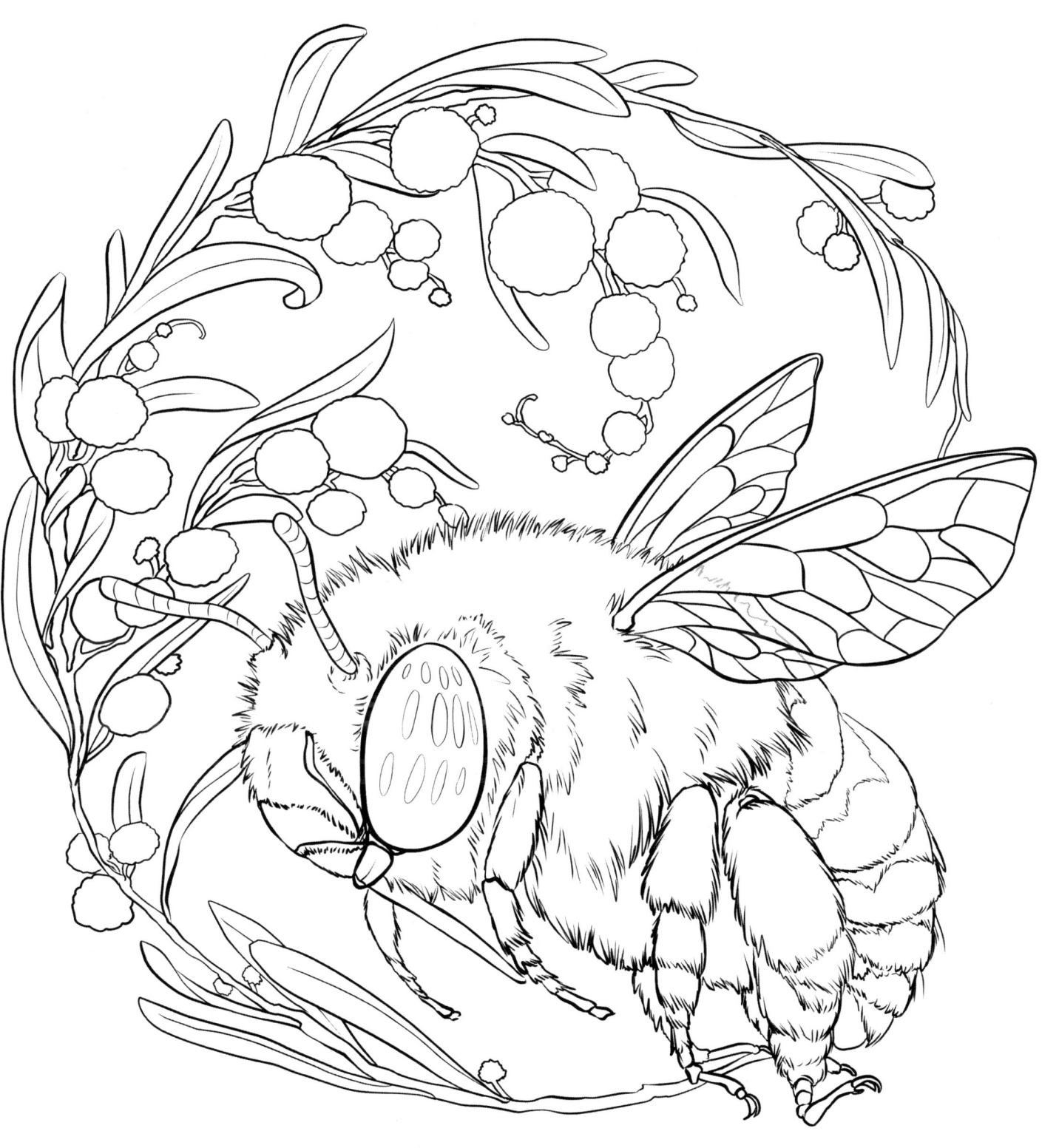

RED-TAILED BLACK COCKATOO AND LEADBEATER'S COCKATOO, WITH TREE ORCHIDS

Although the white and yellow sulphur-crested cockatoo is one of Australia's most famous cockatoos, there are many other species, including this yellow-spotted black cockatoo with red tail stripes, and the pink leadbeater's cockatoo with sunset-striped crest. Tree orchids can be white, pink, or yellow.

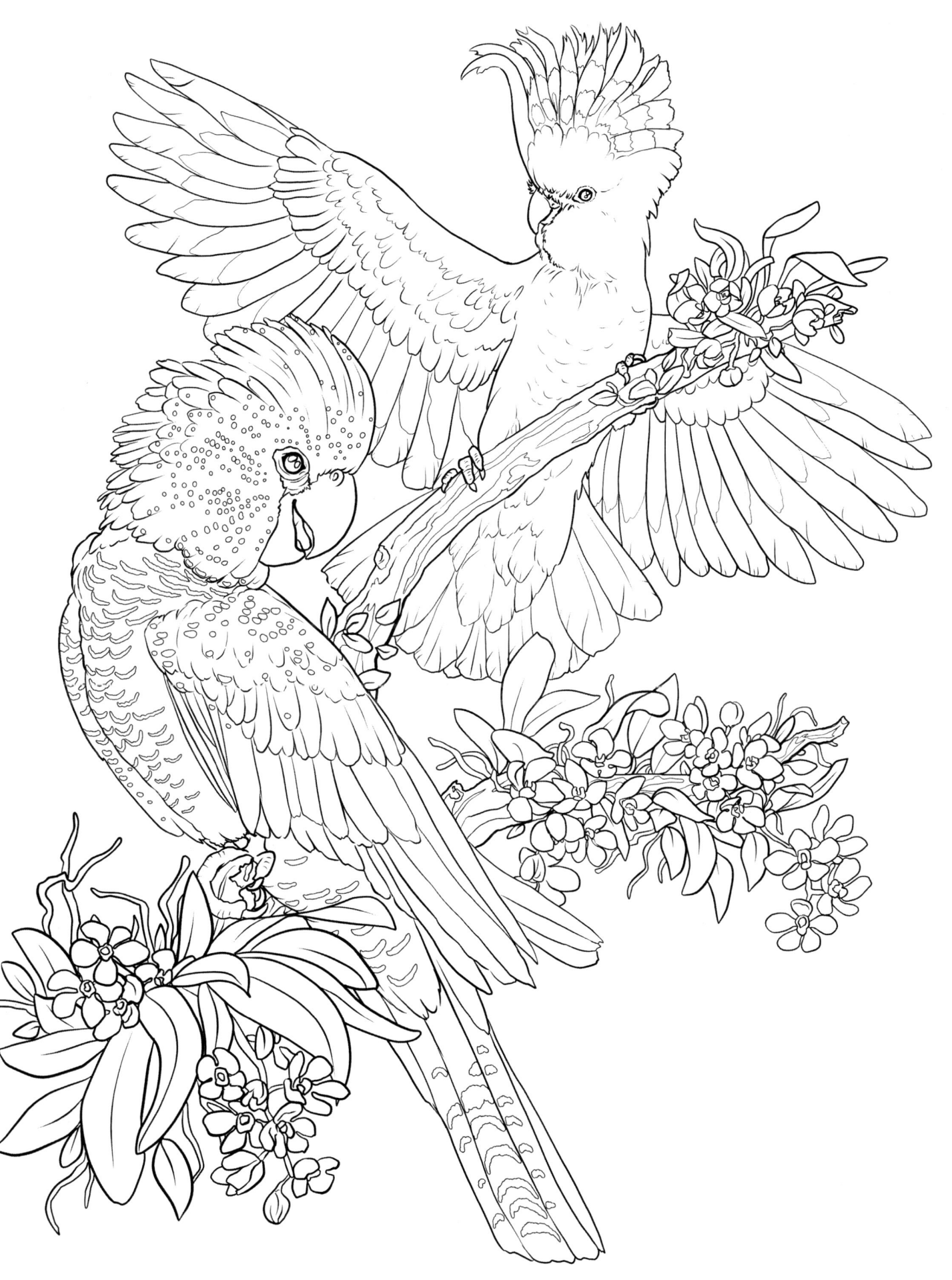

TASMANIAN DEVILS
WITH TASMANIAN WARATAH

The cheeky Tasmanian devil is the largest carnivorous marsupial in the world. All black with white stripes, and pink ears and nose, devils can climb trees and have a bone crushing bite. The Tasmanian species of waratah's flowers are red-to-hot-pink.

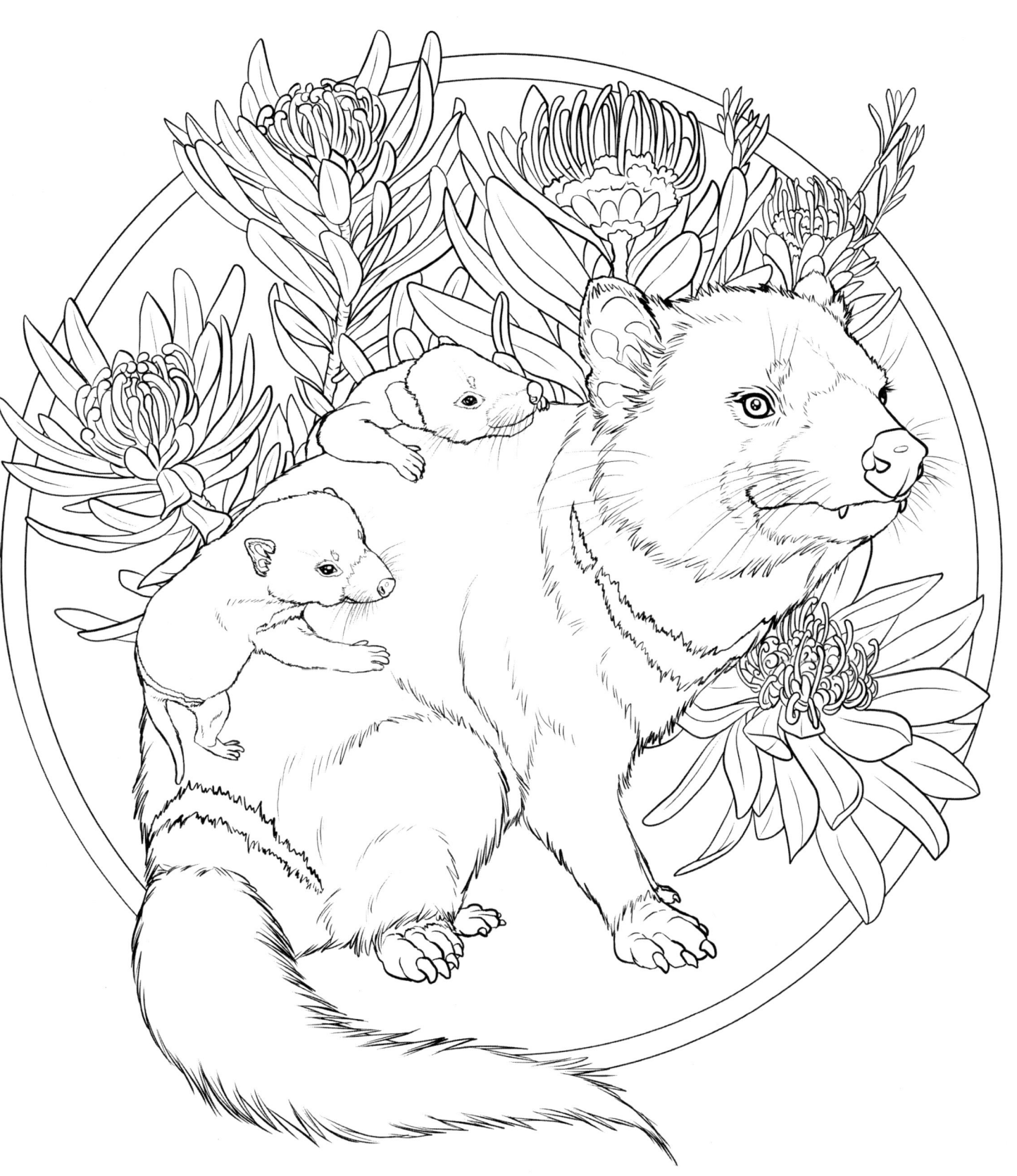

EMUS AND GYMEA LILY

The flightless emu is the world's second largest bird by height, growing up to two metres tall. Eggs and babies are cared for by the male. Gymea lilies have bright red flowers held high above their strappy green leaves on long spears.

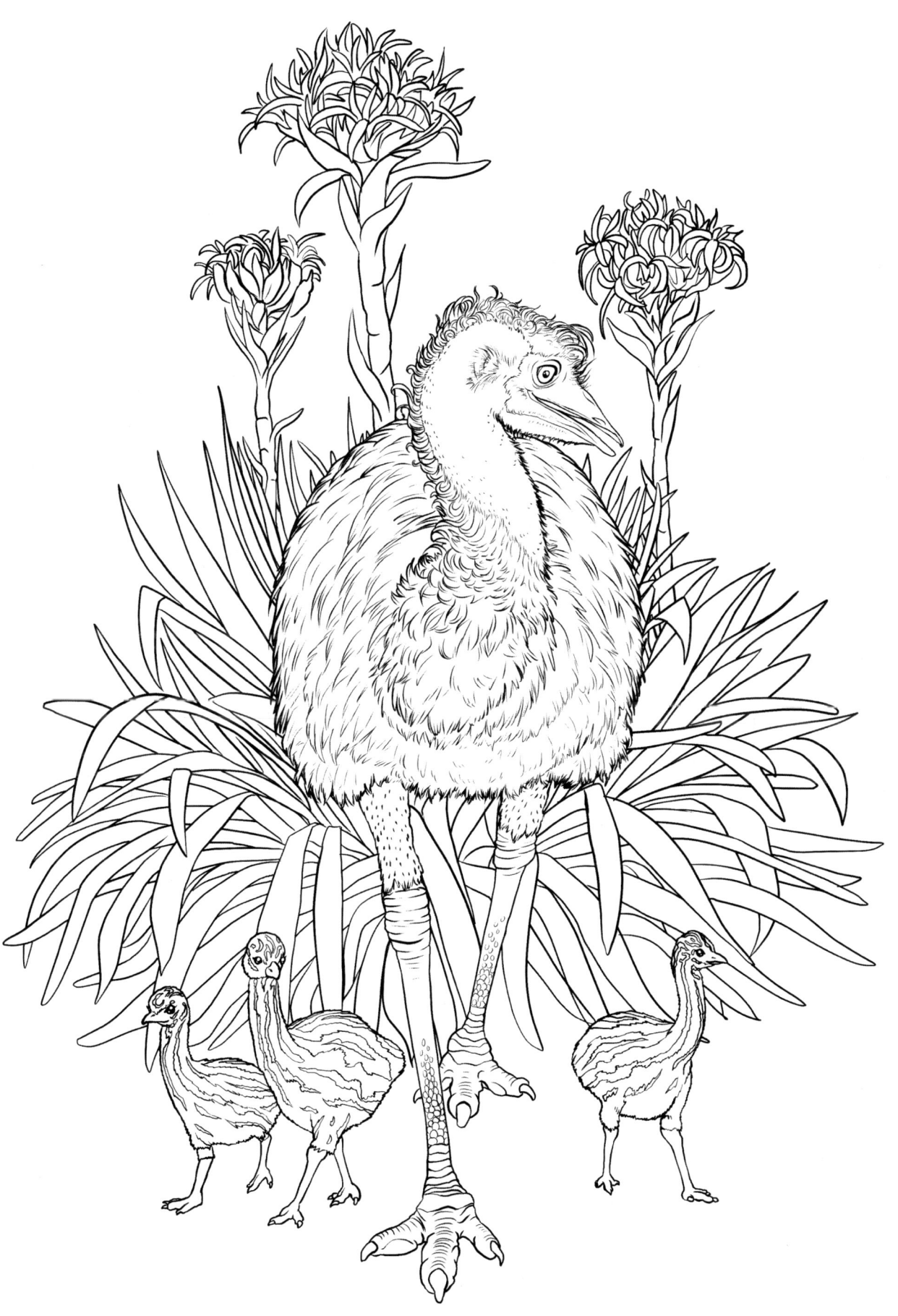

DINGOS AND MOUNTAIN DEVIL

Australia's wild dog, dingos are commonly sandy coloured but can also be black, black and tan, and white. They do not bark, but rather howl like wolves. The mountain devil is a red-flowering shrub that forms pointed seed follicles that resemble devil heads.

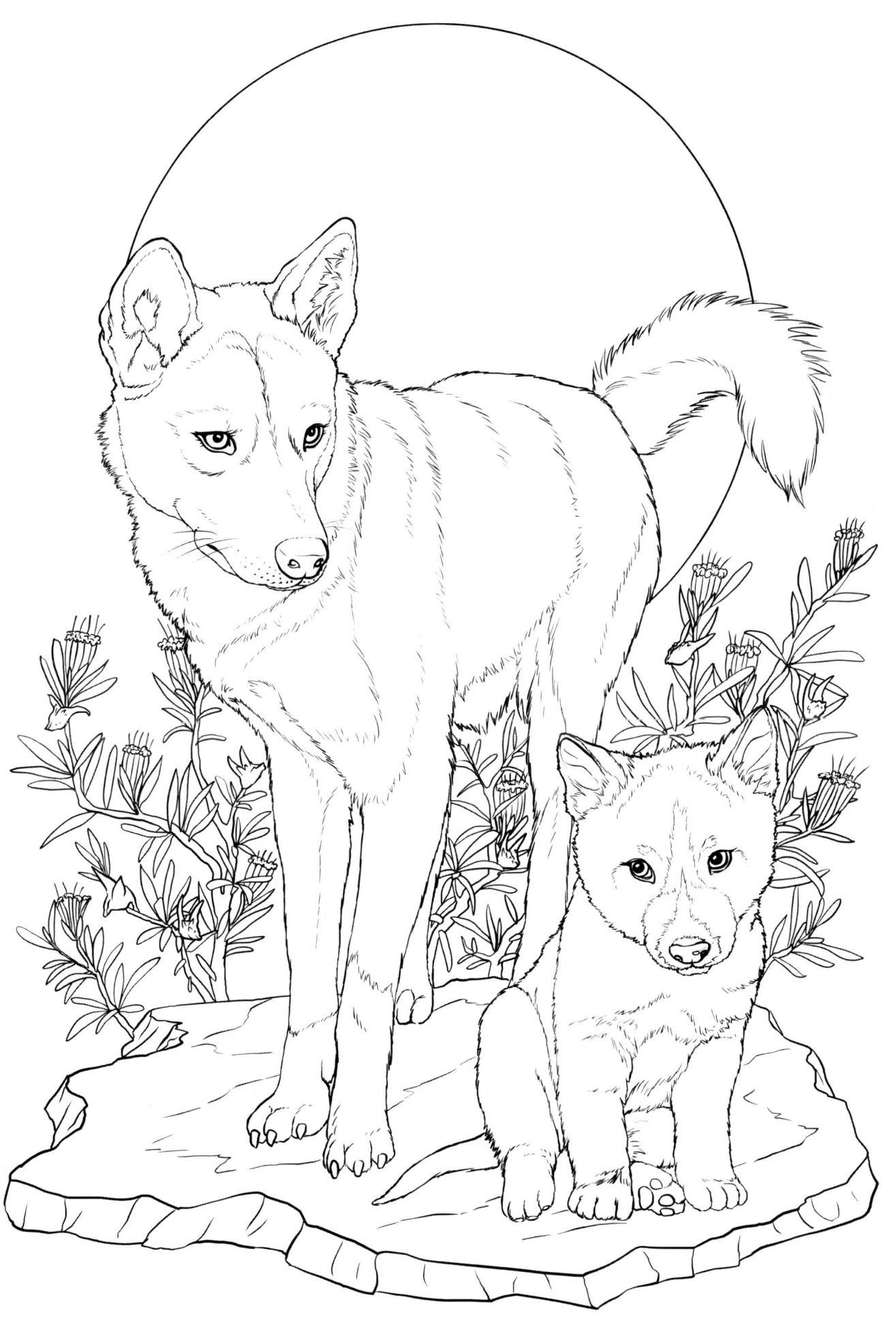

BLUE-WINGED KOOKABURRA AND BANKSIAS

Famous for its laugh, this kookaburra has a white head and chest, brown back and wings with bright blue highlights. There are over 170 species of banksias. Their iconic cylindrical shaped flower spikes come in a range of colours of a vibrant sunset.

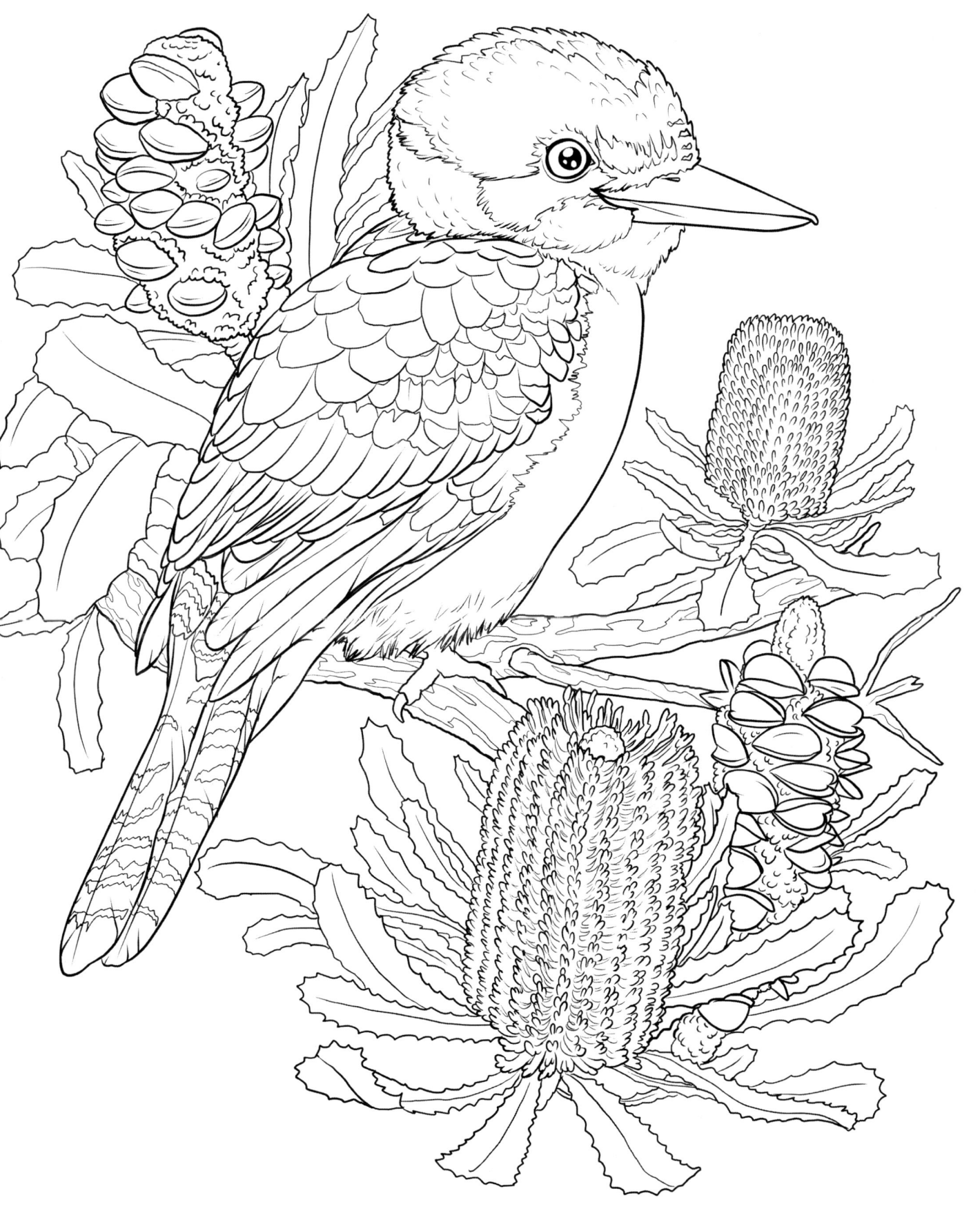

RAKALI WITH RAINBOW NARDOO

Australia's water rat, with rich brown fur and pale yellow-to-orange underside, the rakali recently became famous for being able to eat cane toads without being poisoned. Nardoo is a waterplant related to ferns, which grows in the form of a four-leafed clover. Its leaves range from pale green to rusty-red in tone.

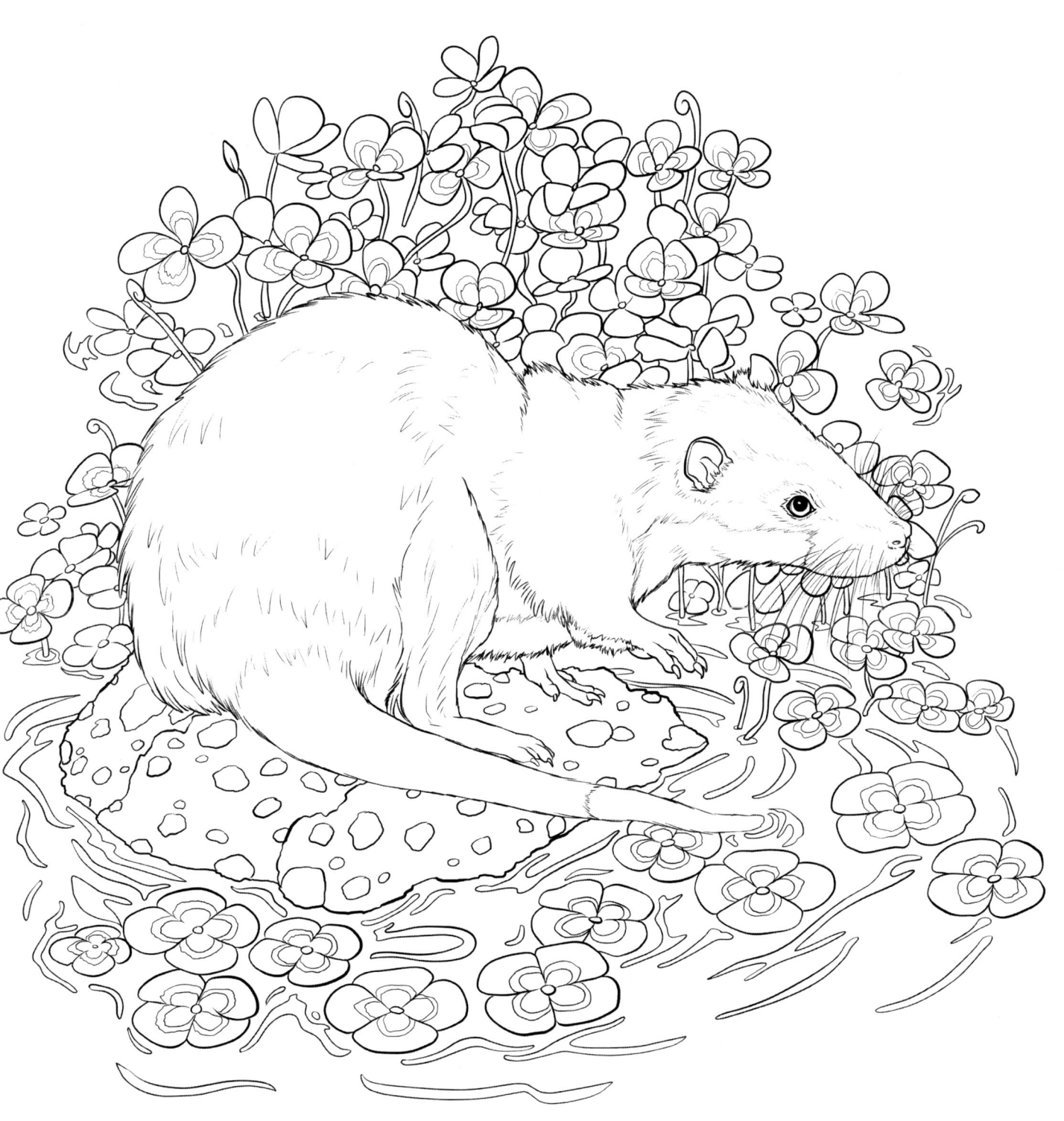

BROLGA WITH CUMBUNGI

Brolgas are famous for their courtship displays, involving elaborate dancing. This pale grey crane has a red head and stands almost human height. Cumbungi are strappy green water plants, most notable for their sausage-like seed head.

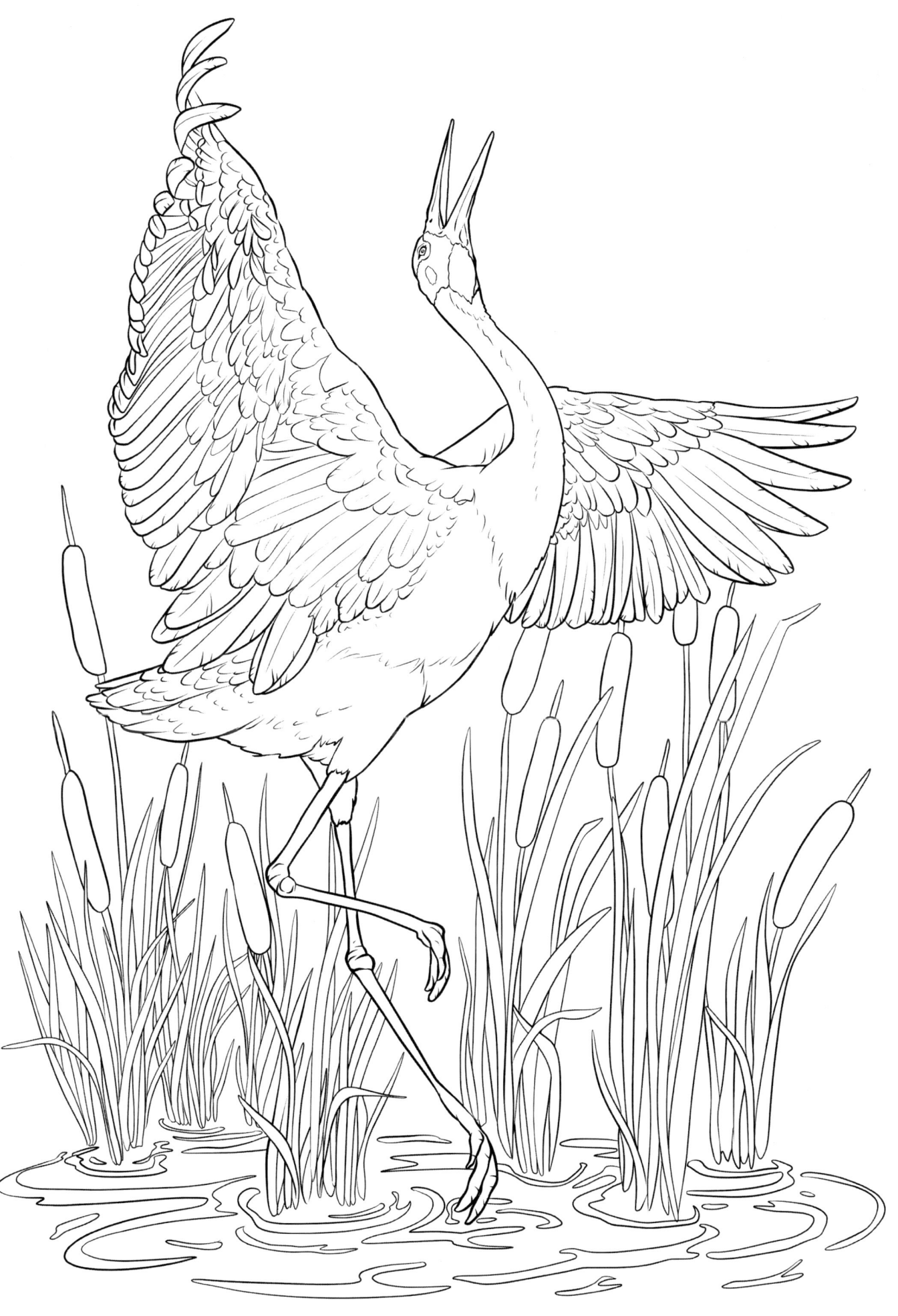

BILBIES AND FLANNEL FLOWERS

Silky, silvery grey bilbies are rabbit-sized and nocturnal. Flannel flowers take their name from the velvety soft feel, with pale green centres and white petals with green tips.

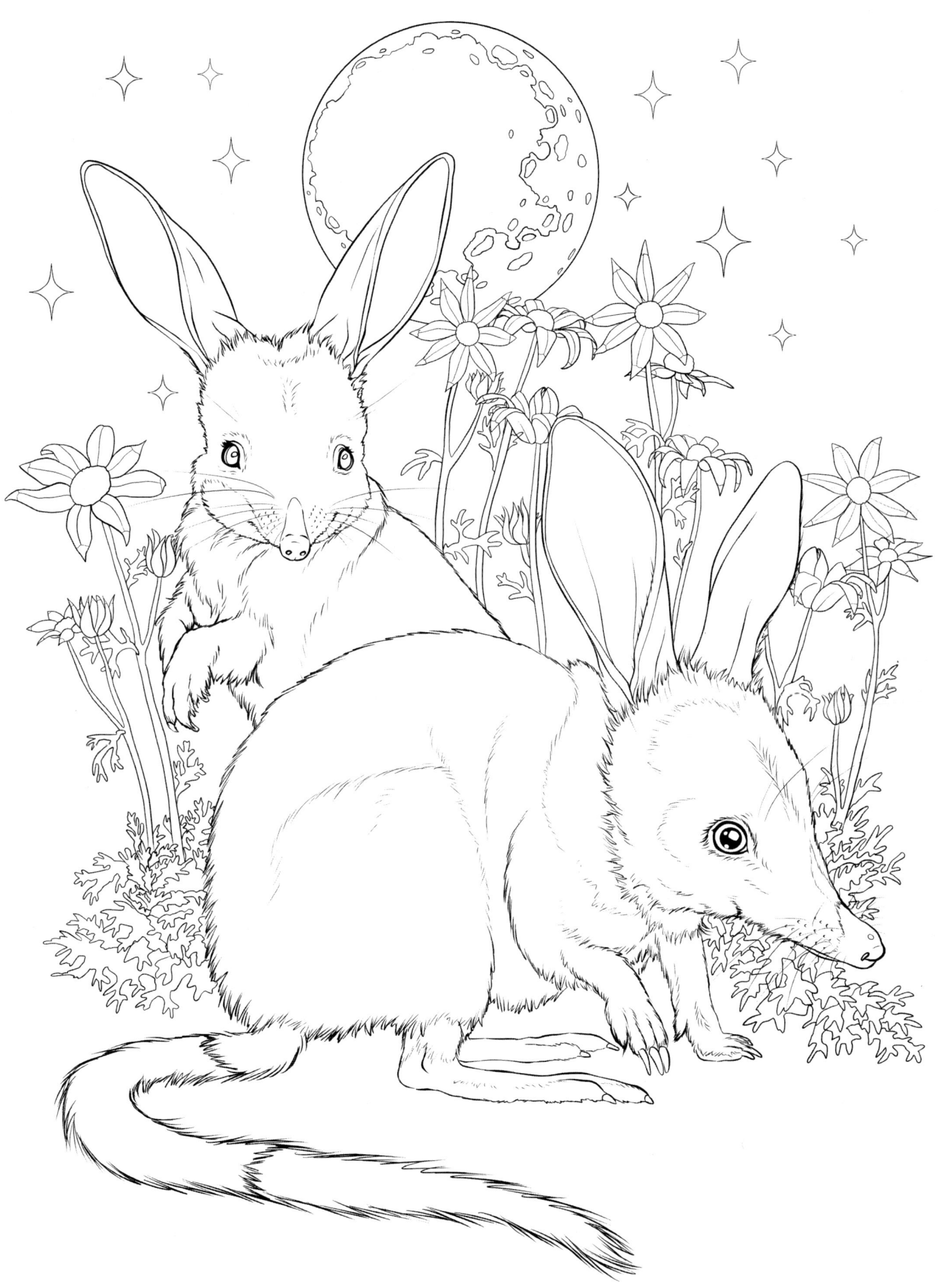

NUMBATS AND CHRISTMAS BELLS

Numbats are insectevorous, eating termites with their long tongues. They have no pouch, rather their babies cling onto the mothers belly. They have russet fur, darkening to black over their rump, with white stripes. Christmas bell flowers are bright red with vibrant yellow tips.

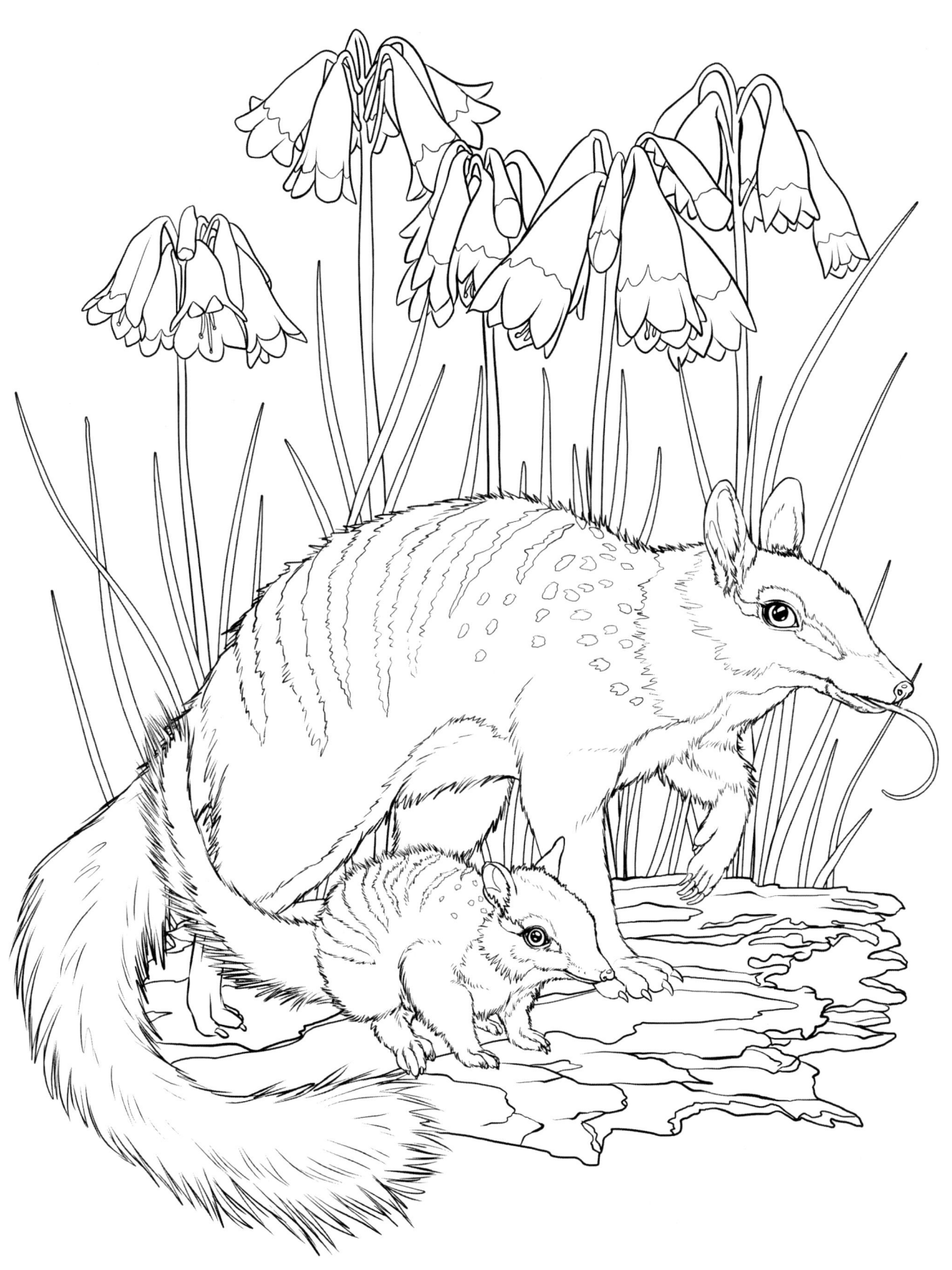

GOANNA WITH STURT'S DESERT PEA

Also known as the lace monitor, goannas can grow over two metres long. Their patterned scales in yellows and blacks provide camouflage, and they swallow their prey whole. Sturt's desert pea is most famously bright red with a black centre, but can also be pink and white.

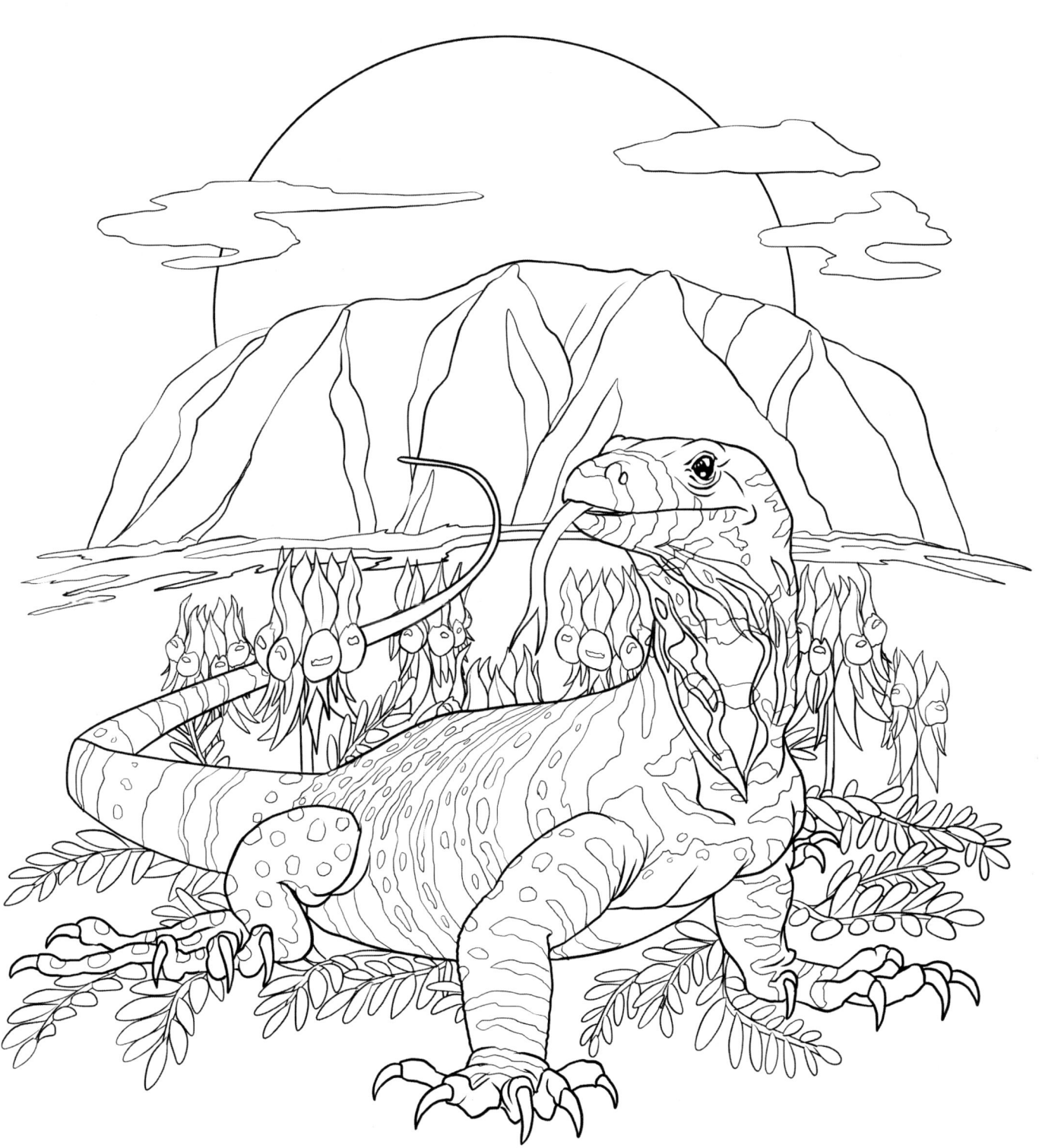

GREY-HEADED FLYING FOXES WITH LILLY PILLY

Flying foxes, or fruit bats, live in large communities. They have large black wings, rusty-red neck fur and grey heads. Lilly pillies grow multitudes of pink fruits, and often have pink and red tipped leaves.

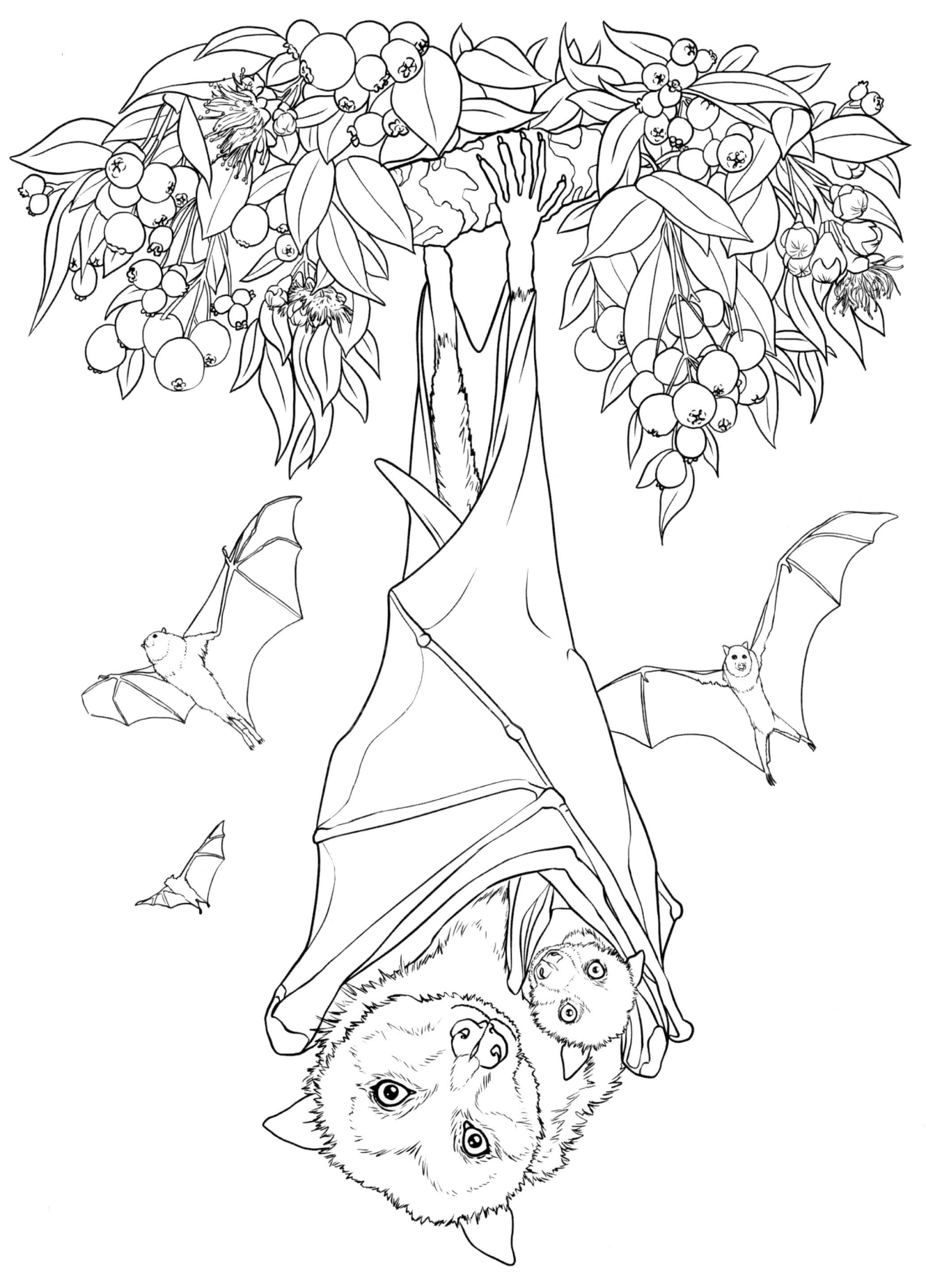

GOLDEN BELL FROG AND ALBANY PITCHER PLANTS

This green and gold coloured frog is one of Australia's largest, growing up to eleven centimetres long. The bright green and red jug-shaped traps of the Albany pitcher plant lure in insects which it eats.

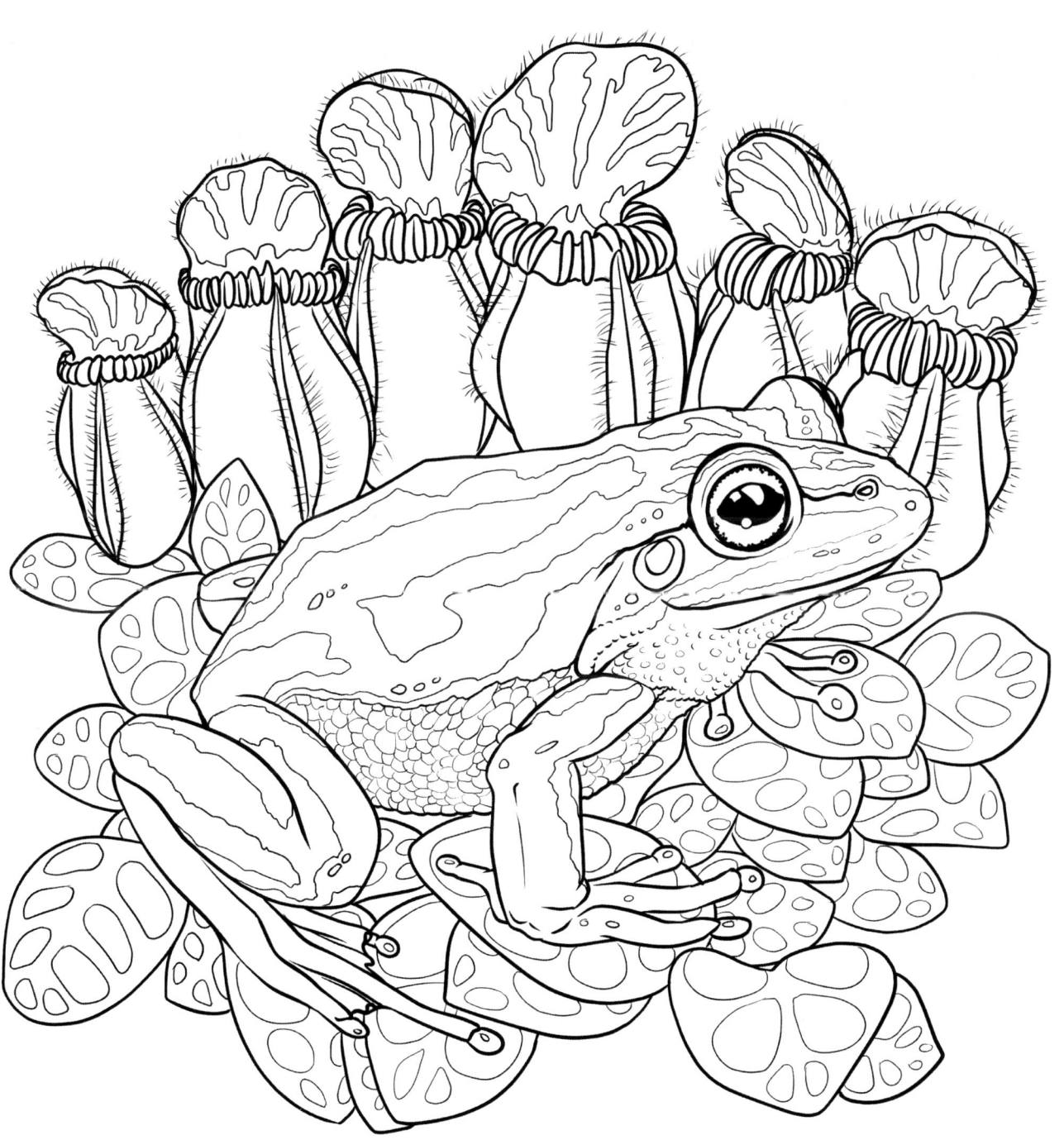

SUGAR GLIDER WITH LACEBARK KURRAJONG

Pale grey with cream belly and black stripes, the sugar glider is a tiny marsupial. It has the ability to glide using mebranes which stretch between its wrists and ankles. The lacebark kurrajong is a large tree with bright pink flowers.

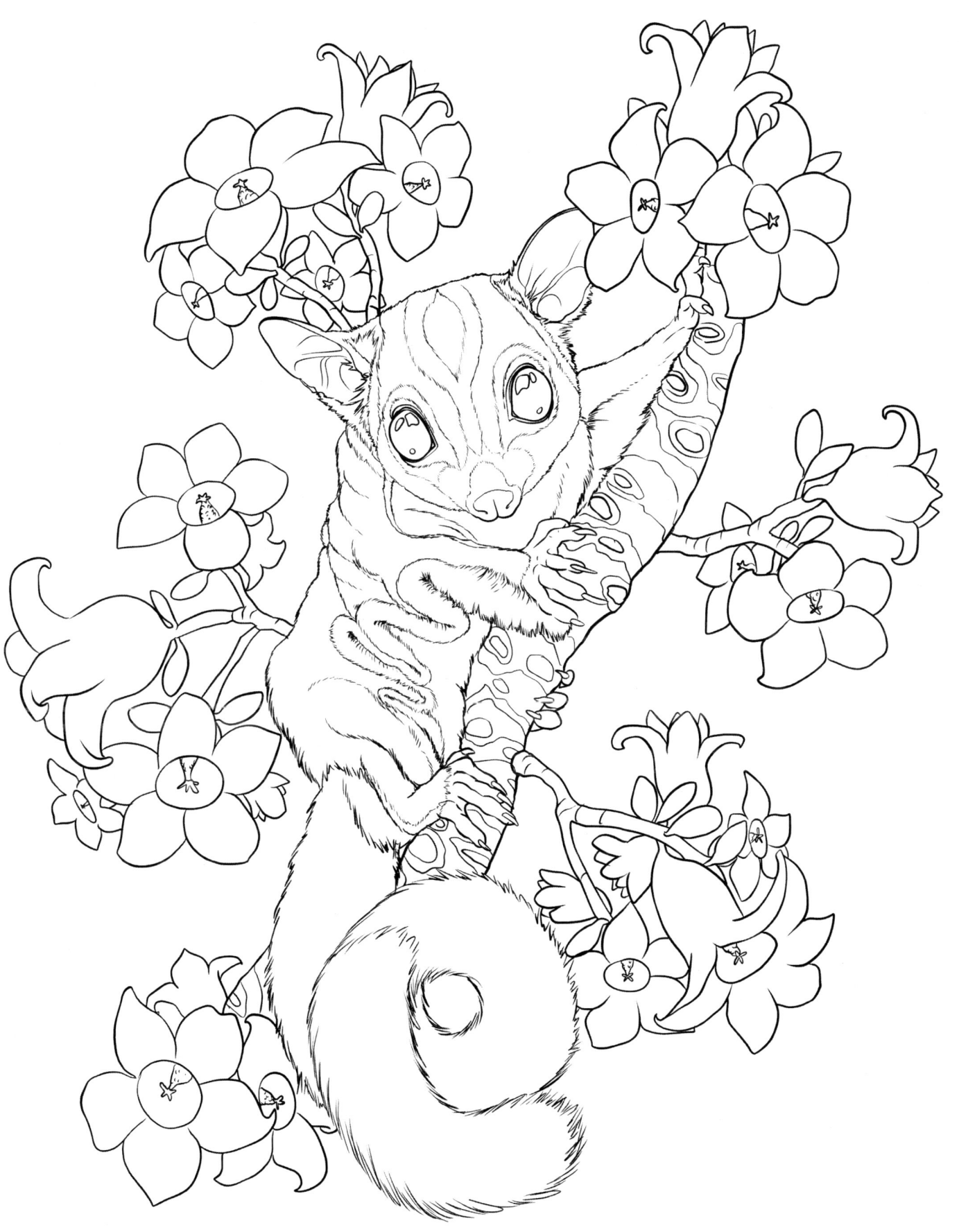

BEARDED DRAGON AND BLUE DAMPIERA

These lizards appear in a range of stone and earth colours, from warm orange to charcoal grey, and can grow up to 55 centimetres in length. They will enlarge their spikey throats when threatened.
The blue dampiera is a small wildflower with striking blue blossoms.

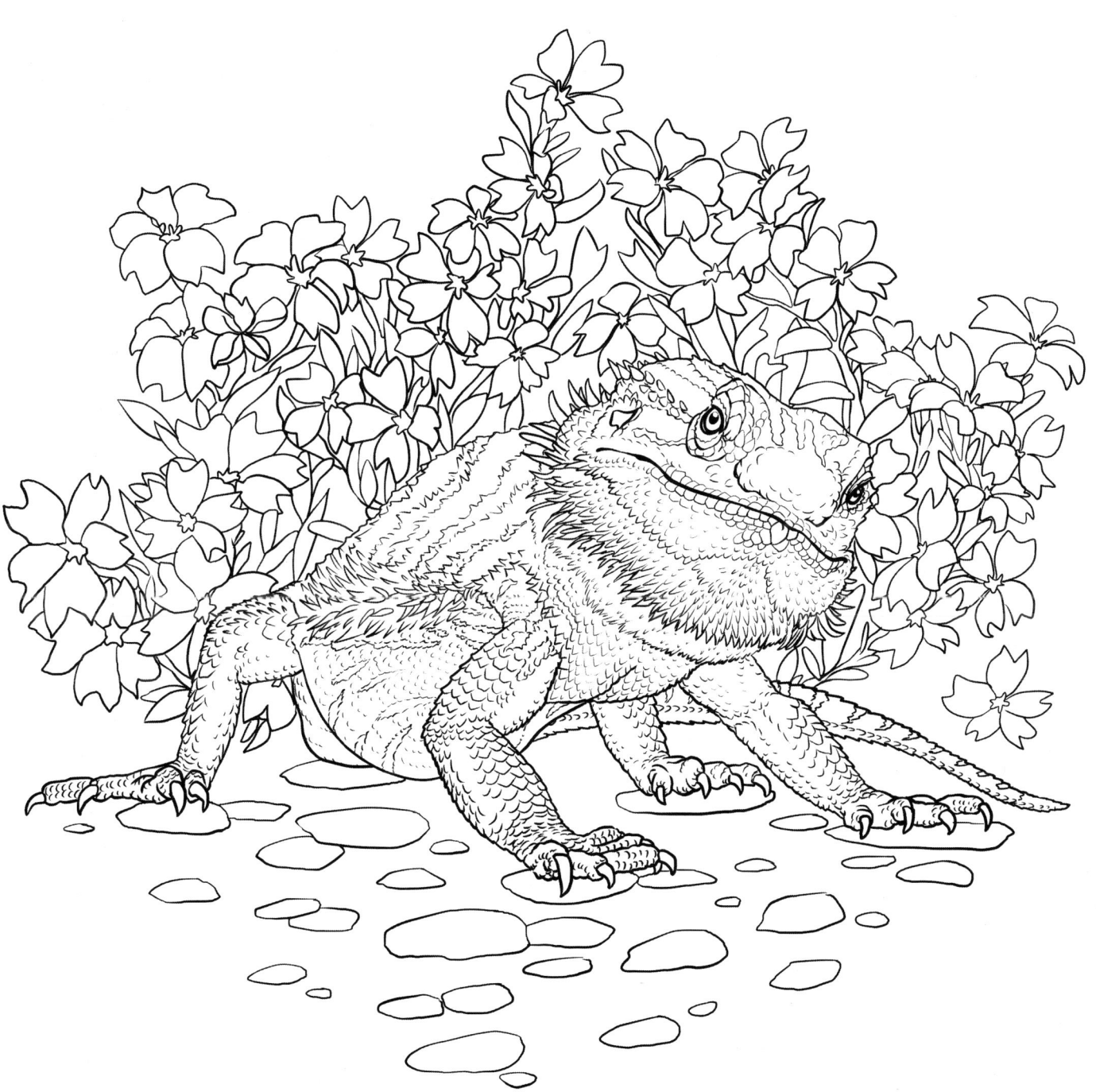

CORROBOREE FROGS AND SUNDEWS

These boldly patterned black and yellow frogs are small enough to fit on the tip of your finger. Sundew's bright green and red leaves are covered in tiny hairs with sticky mucilage, designed to trap insects on which this plant feeds.

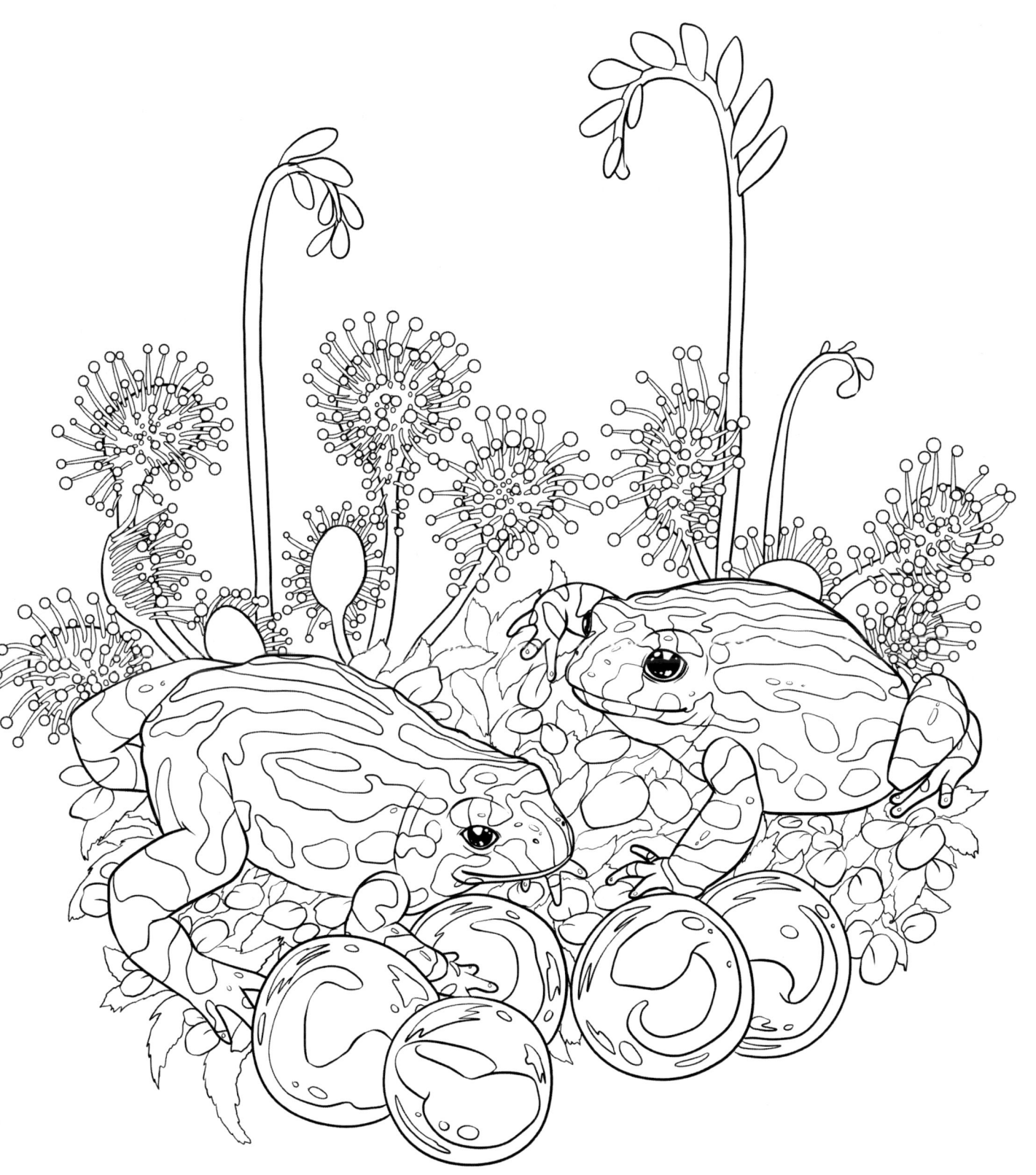

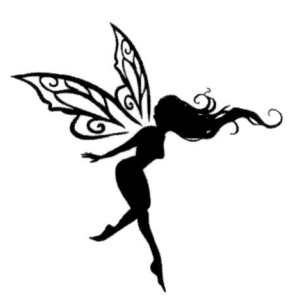

Second Set of Pages Begins Here

When designing my books I decided to print them with two copies of each design, because as an artist I know there are always so many possibilities! I also wanted to give everybody the chance of a do-over with every design in case of an oops (as an artist I know that happens too!). Try a different medium, or a different colour scheme. Create without fear! Or share the magic with a loved one. Because sharing your creativity and joy of color is the best magic of all. ~ *Selina*

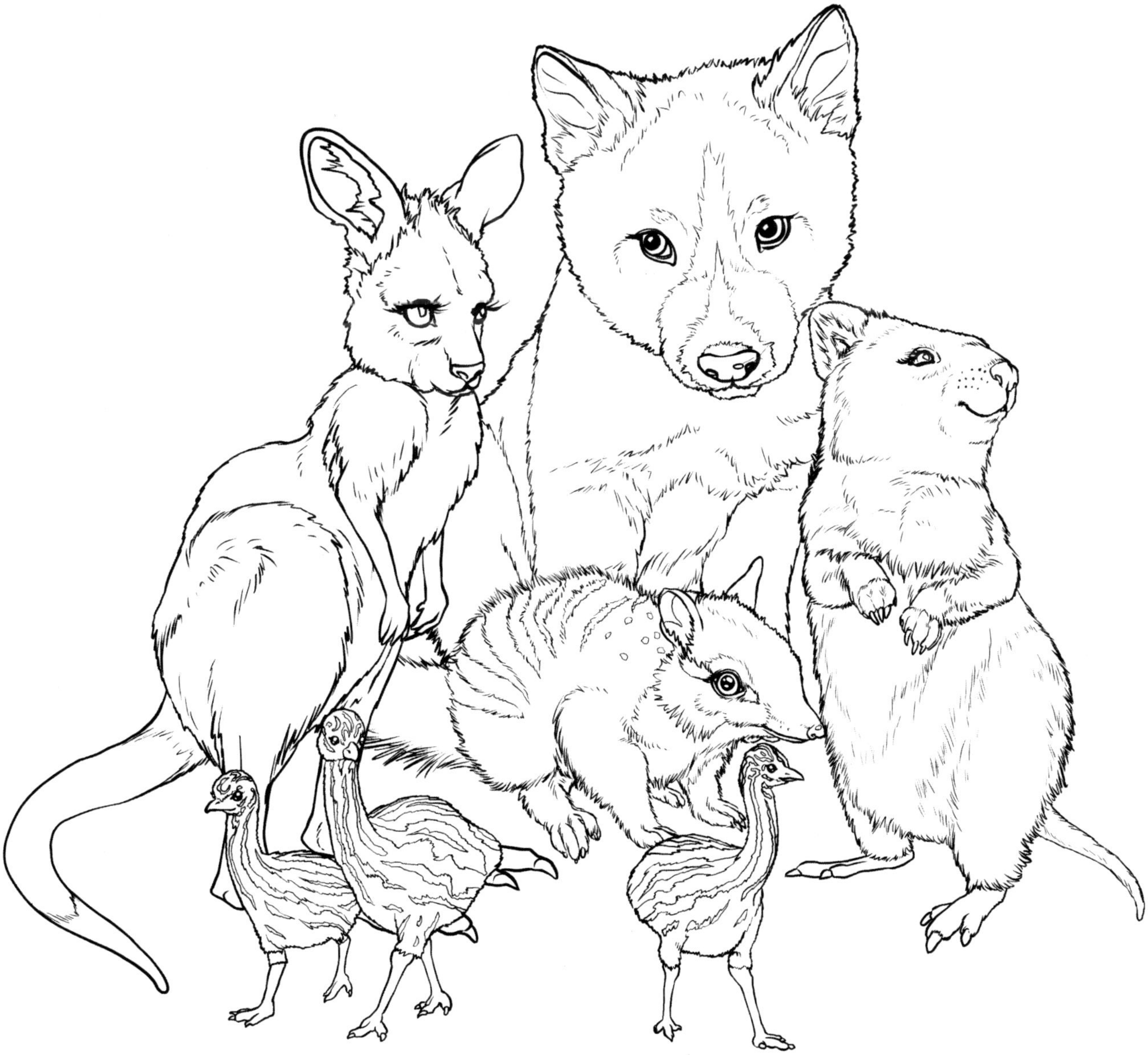

WALLABIES AND WARATAH

Related to kangaroos, but generally smaller, these macropods also carry their joeys in a pouch. Waratah flowers are most famously bright red, but can also be white, pink, or yellow.

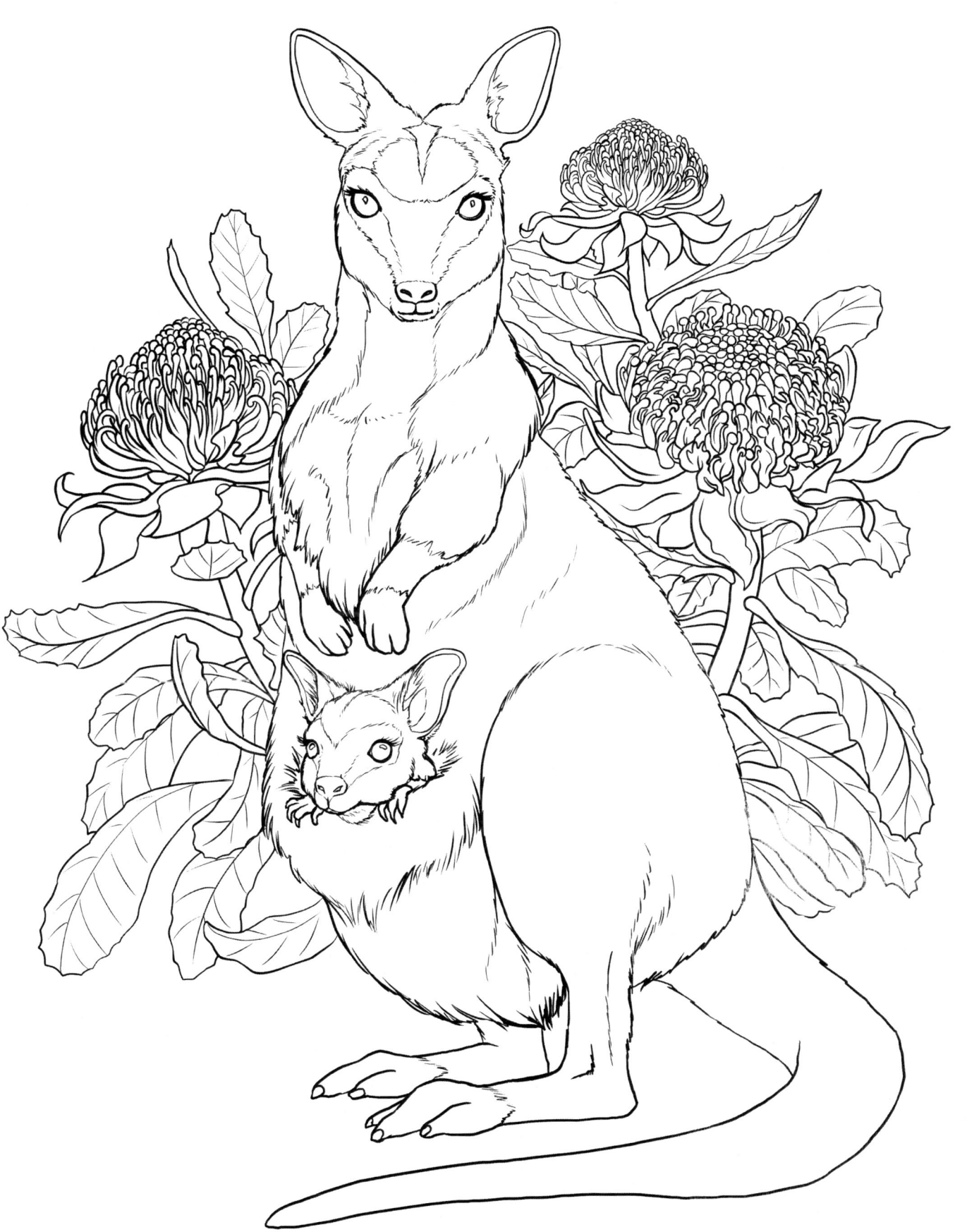

WOMBATS AND STRAWFLOWERS

Wombats, like most marsupials, have pouches, however their pouch faces backwards to avoid filling with dirt while they dig their burrows. Strawflowers are also known as everlasting daisies because their straw-like texture means they make beautiful dried flowers. Commonly yellow, but also appear in a range of pinks and white.

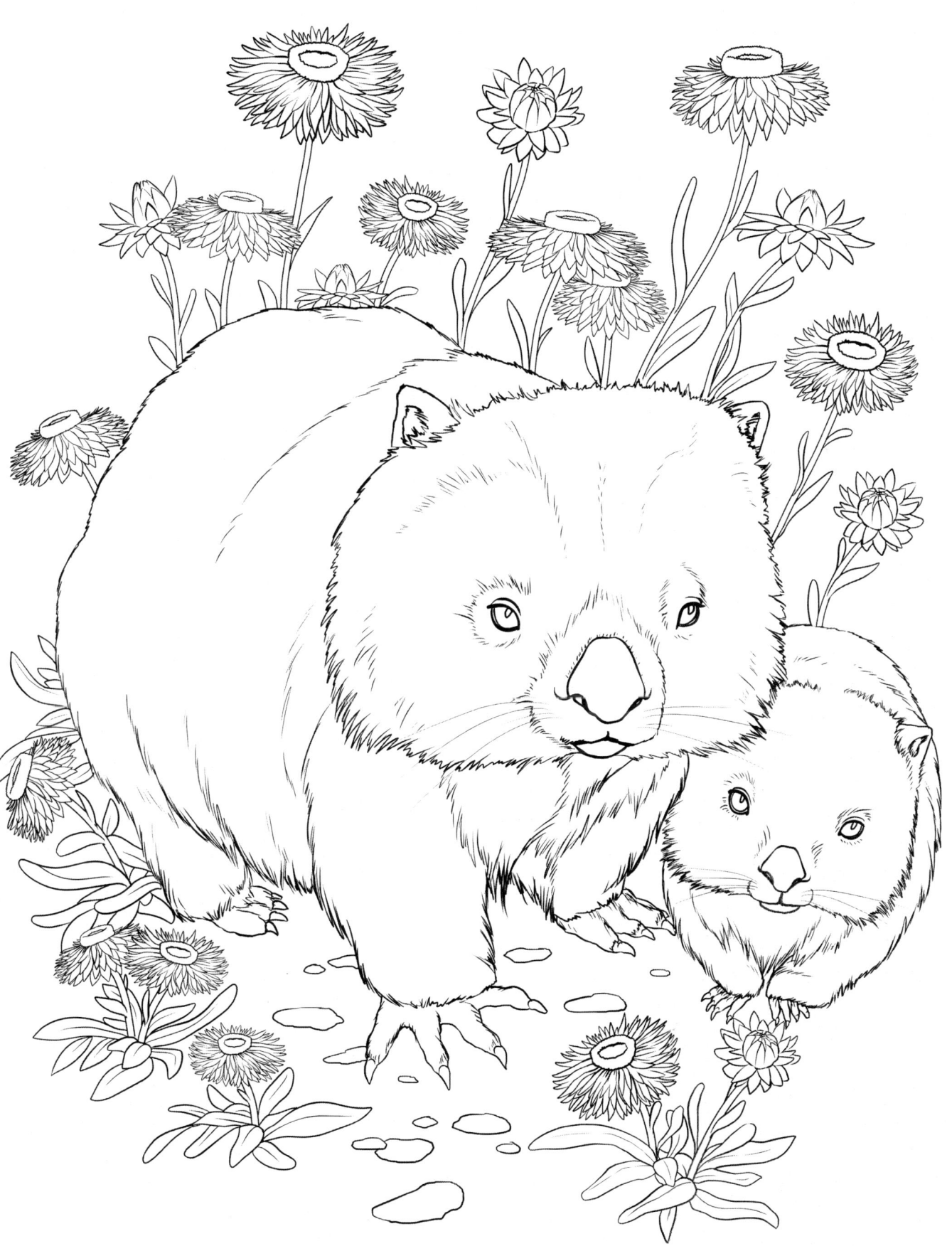

GREY KANGAROOS WITH KANGAROO PAW FLOWER

One of Australia's most iconic animals, known for their hopping motion and for carrying their joeys in a pouch. The Kangaroo Paw flower is named for its flower's resemblance to paws. The flowers come in many striking colours.

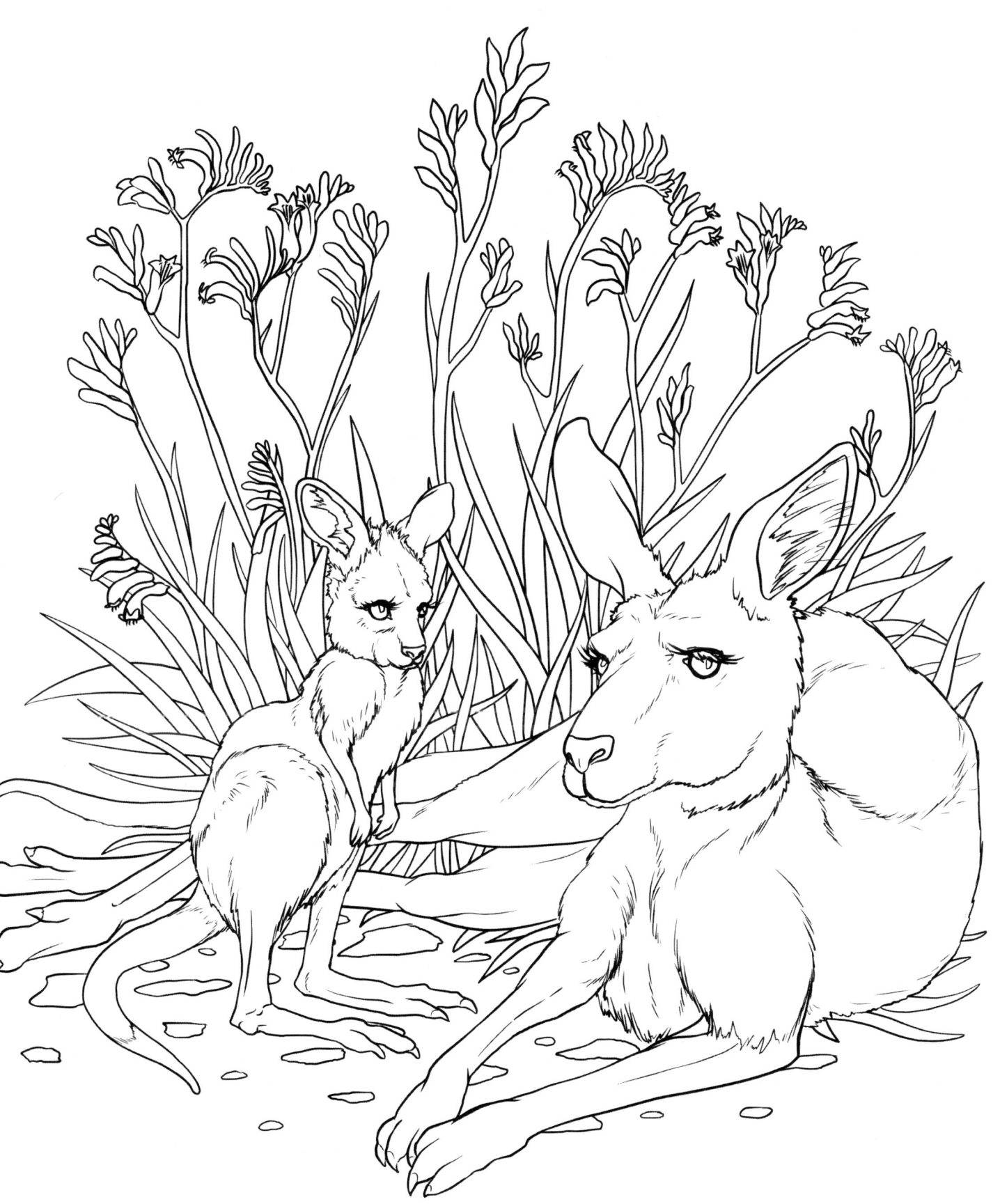

KOALAS AND EUCALYPTUS

Australia's favourite fluffy animal, Koala's feed almost exclusively on eucalyptus leaves, which are toxic to most other animals. Koalas have two opposable thumbs on each hand for better climbing. Eucalyptus (or gum tree) blossoms are commonly white, yellow, pink, or red.

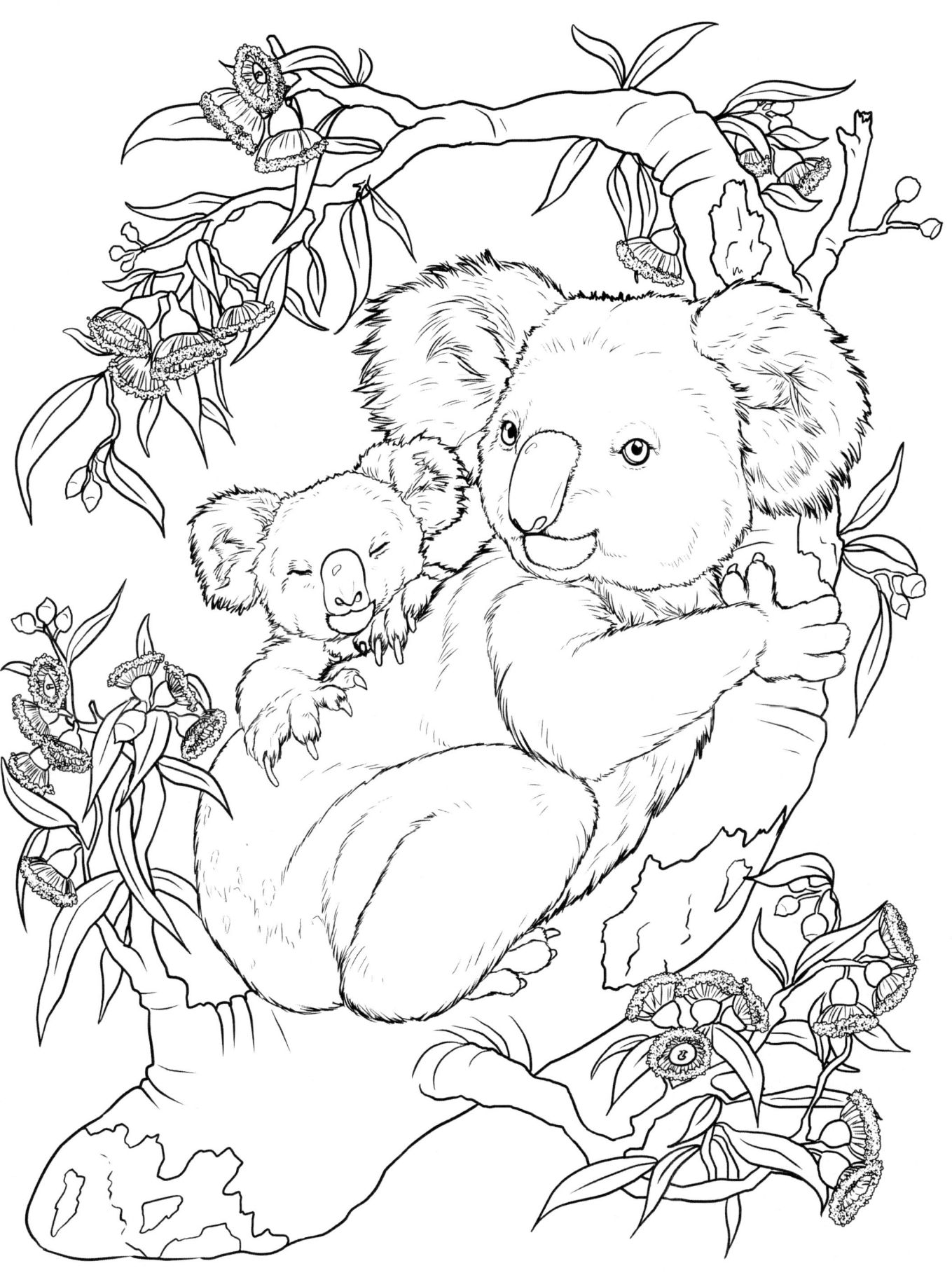

ECHIDNA WITH COWSLIP ORCHID, FLYING DUCK ORCHID, AND SNAKE ORCHID

The bizarre echidna is one of the world's only two monotremes - warm blooded, milk producing animals that lay eggs. They eat ants and insects with their long tongues. Cowslip and snake orchids have yellow flowers, while the flying duck orchid is a deep maroon, and shaped like tiny flying ducks.

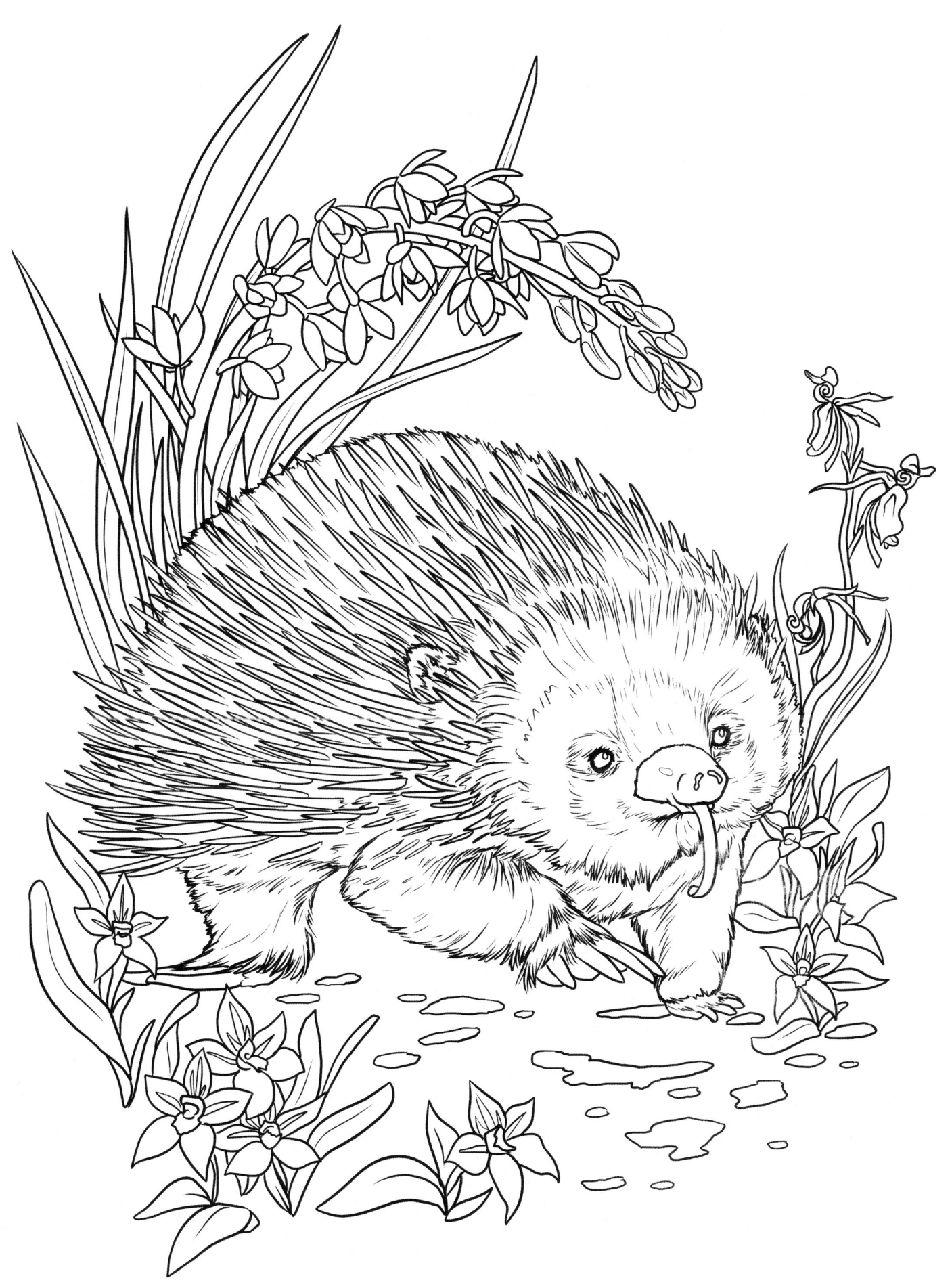

PLATYPUS WITH WATERLILIES AND NYMPHOIDES FRINGE LILY.

One of only two monotremes in the world, the Platypus is an egg laying mammal. With its duck-like bill and webbed feet, early reports of its existence by British colonists were considered to be hoaxes. Fringe lilies flower in white or yellow, while Australian varieties of water lily are generally lilac.

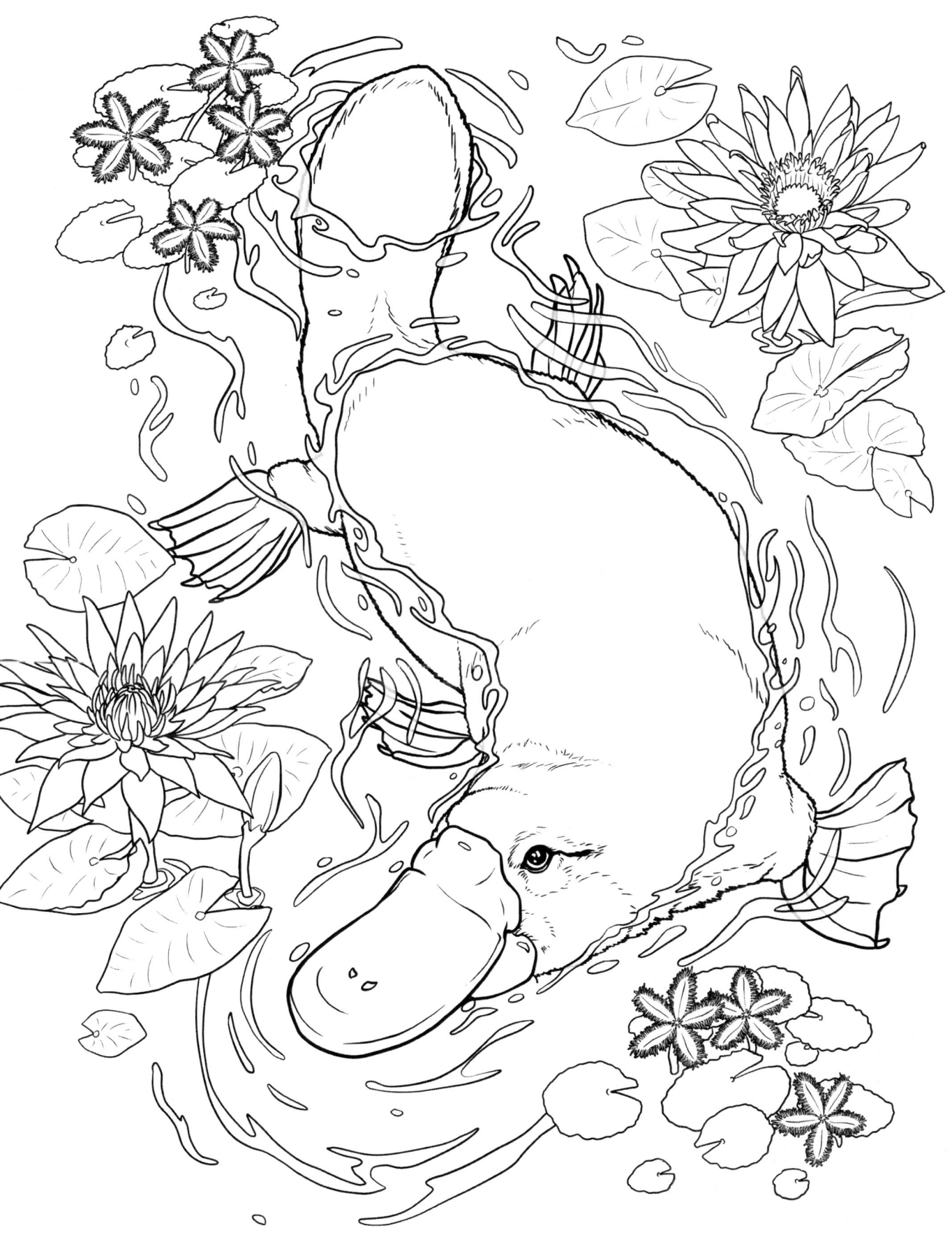

QUOKKAS AND COMMON HEATH

Famous for being Australia's happiest animal, quokkas are part of the macropod family along with kangaroos and wallabies. The common heath is a prickly bush covered in masses of pink, bell-shaped flowers.

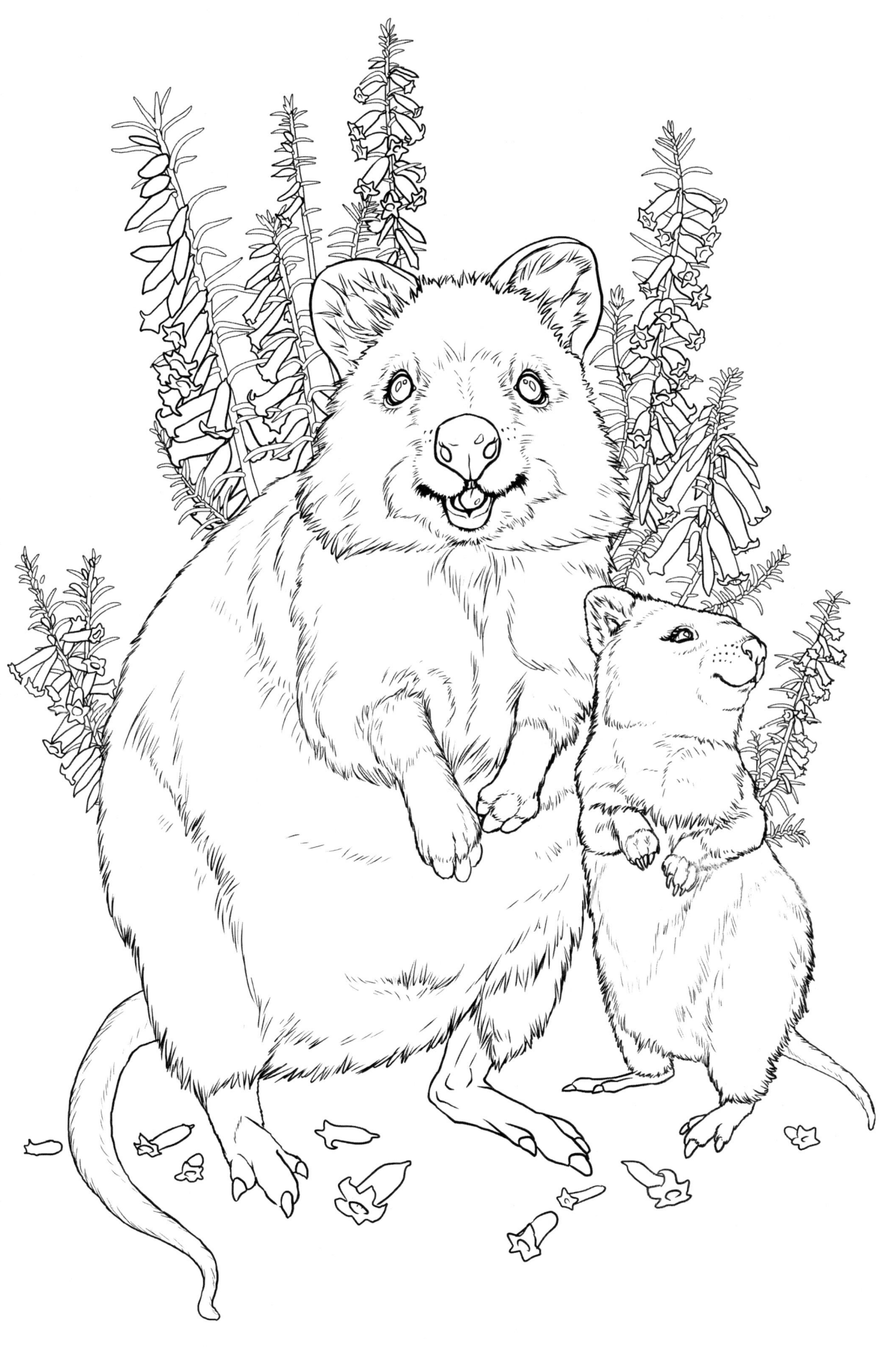

QUOLLS AND CROWEAS

Quolls are a catlike, carnivorous marsupial. Its babies are the size of a grain of rice when born, and will sometimes piggy-back on their mother once they are too large for the pouch. Some quoll species only develop a pouch during breeding season. Crowea's star-like flowers come in violet, pink, or white.

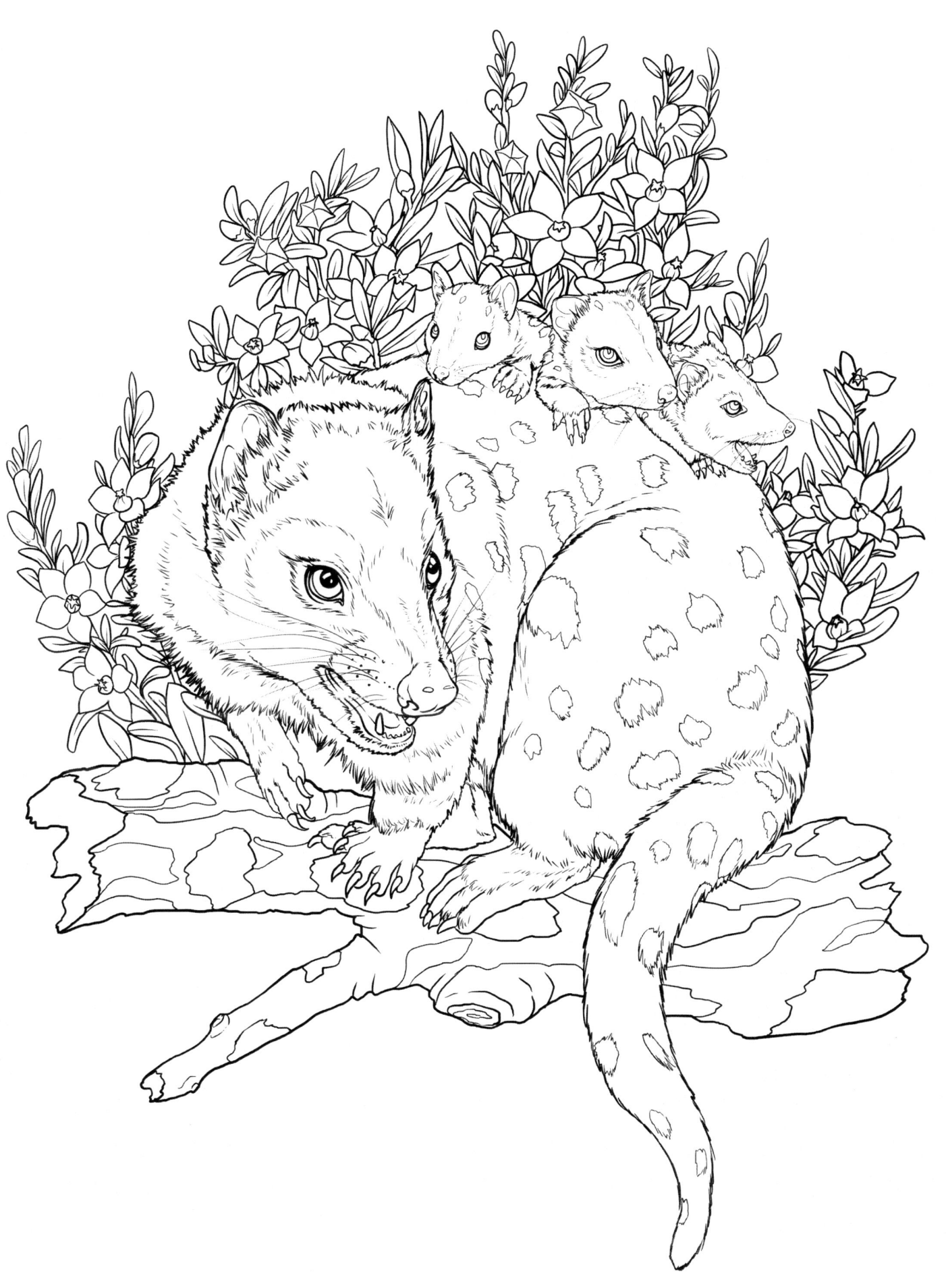

RAINBOW LORIKEETS WITH GREVILLEA

This particularly cheeky, vibrant, rainbow coloured bird feeds on fruits and nectar. Grevilleas come in a multitude of varieties, and (like the lorikeet) in many colours of the rainbow.

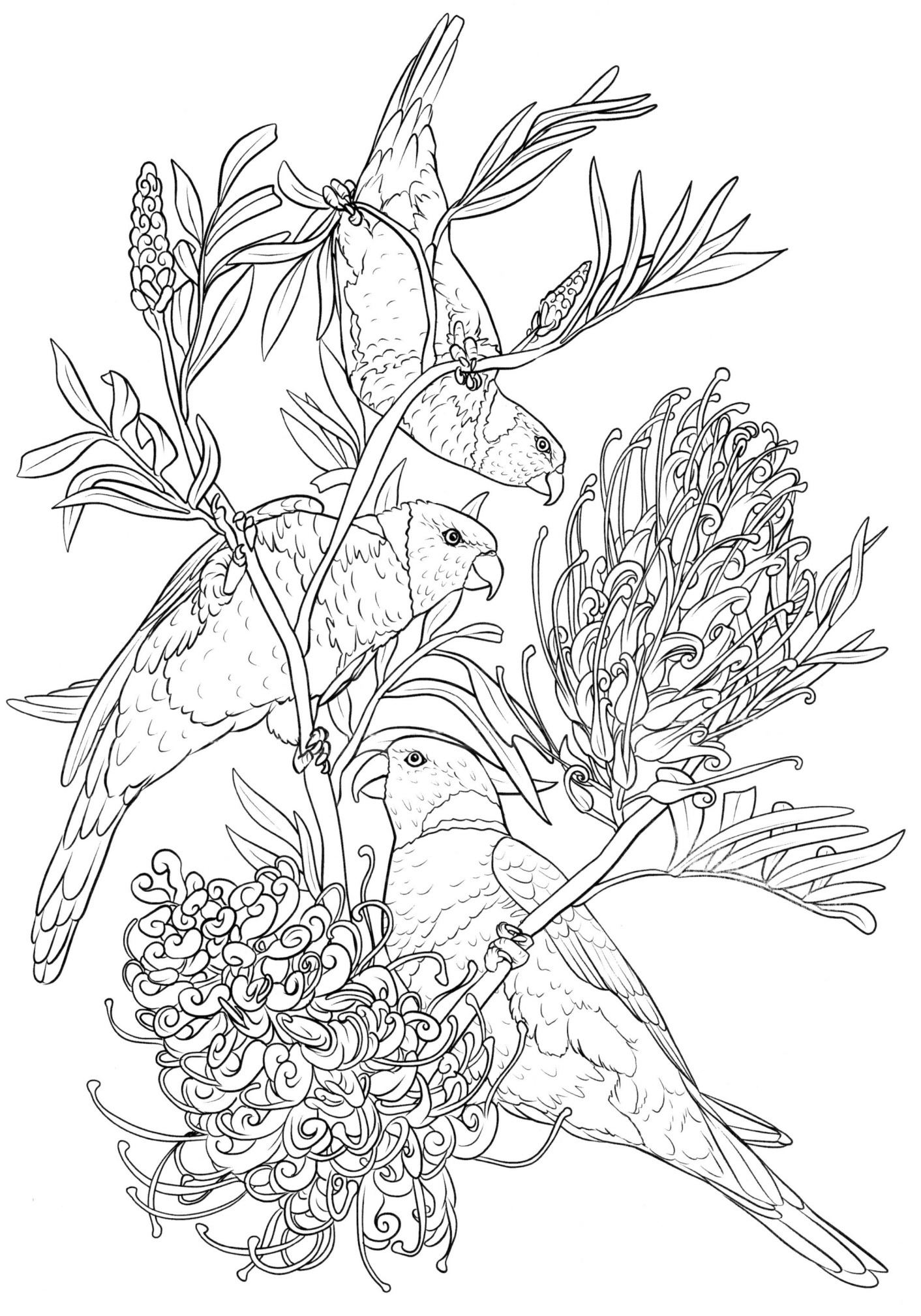

BLUE BANDED BEE WITH WATTLE

Blue banded bees have fluffy orange fur on their thorax, with black and blue stripes on their abdomen. They are solitary, and while they have a sting they aren't agressive. There are many varieties of wattle with flowers of different shapes, but all are similar in their iconic stunning bright yellow.

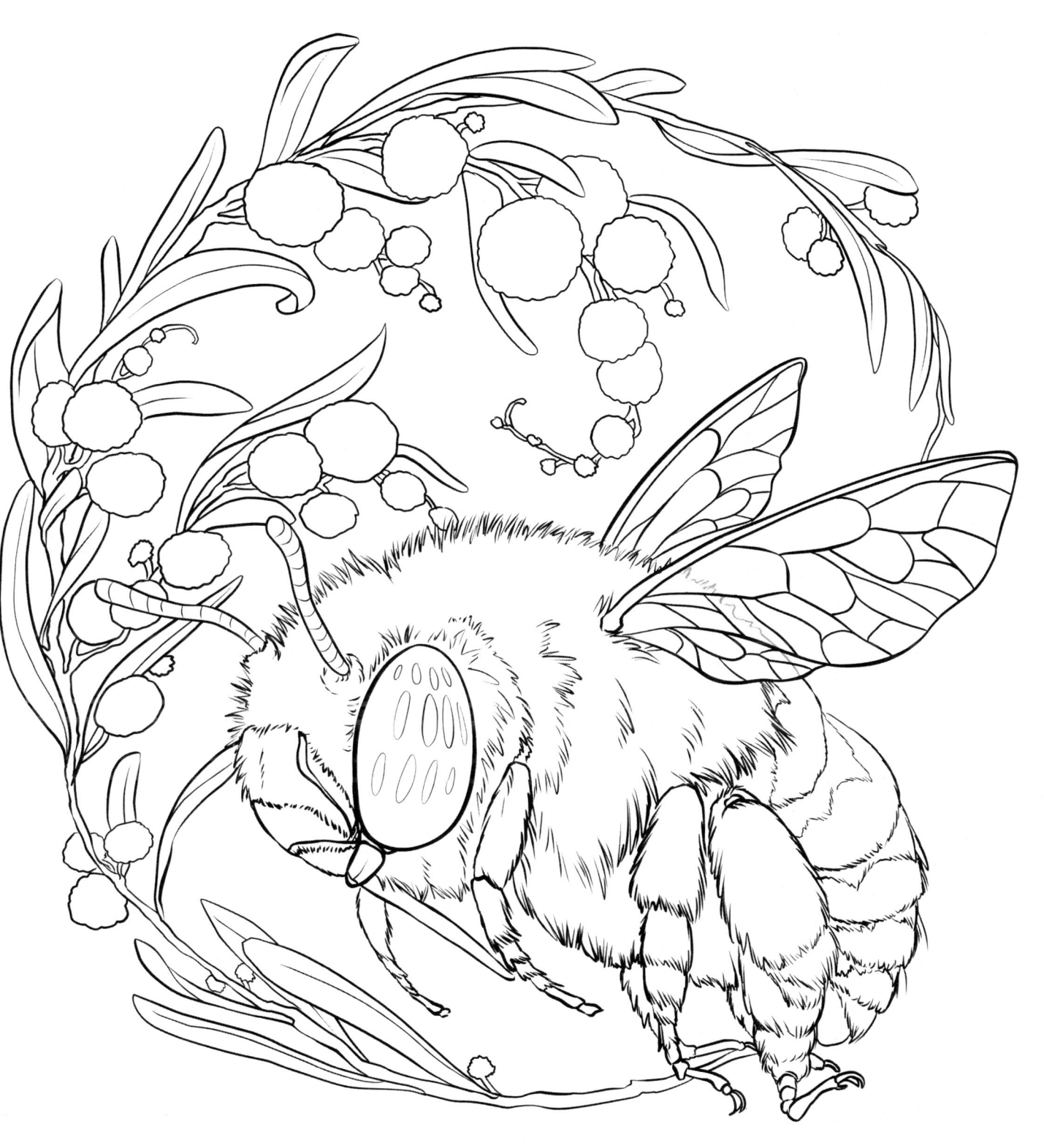

RED-TAILED BLACK COCKATOO AND LEADBEATER'S COCKATOO, WITH TREE ORCHIDS

Although the white and yellow sulphur-crested cockatoo is one of Australia's most famous cockatoos, there are many other species, including this yellow-spotted black cockatoo with red tail stripes, and the pink leadbeater's cockatoo with sunset-striped crest. Tree orchids can be white, pink, or yellow.

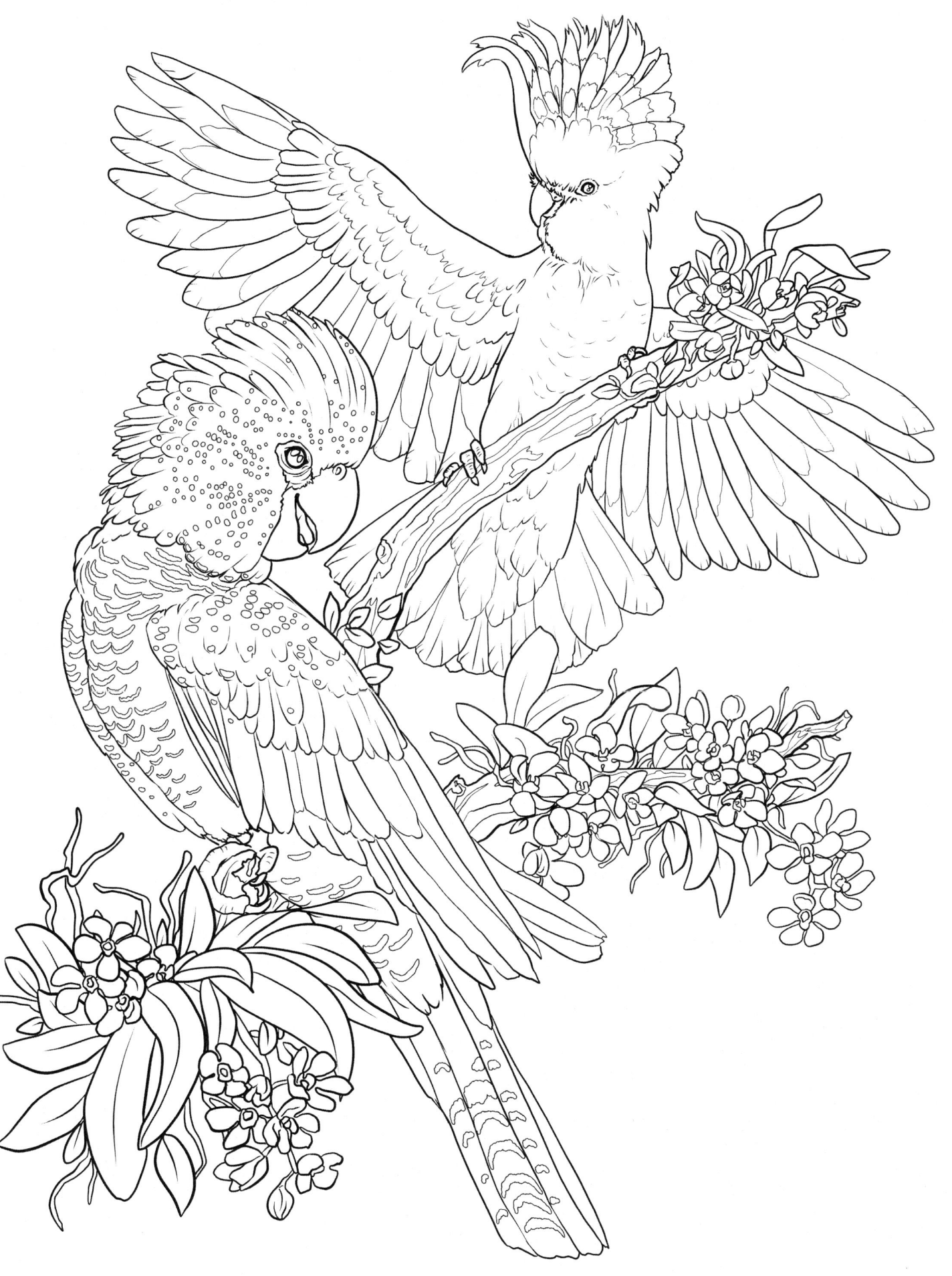

TASMANIAN DEVILS
WITH TASMANIAN WARATAH

The cheeky Tasmanian devil is the largest carnivorous marsupial in the world. All black with white stripes, and pink ears and nose, devils can climb trees and have a bone crushing bite. The Tasmanian species of waratah's flowers are red-to-hot-pink.

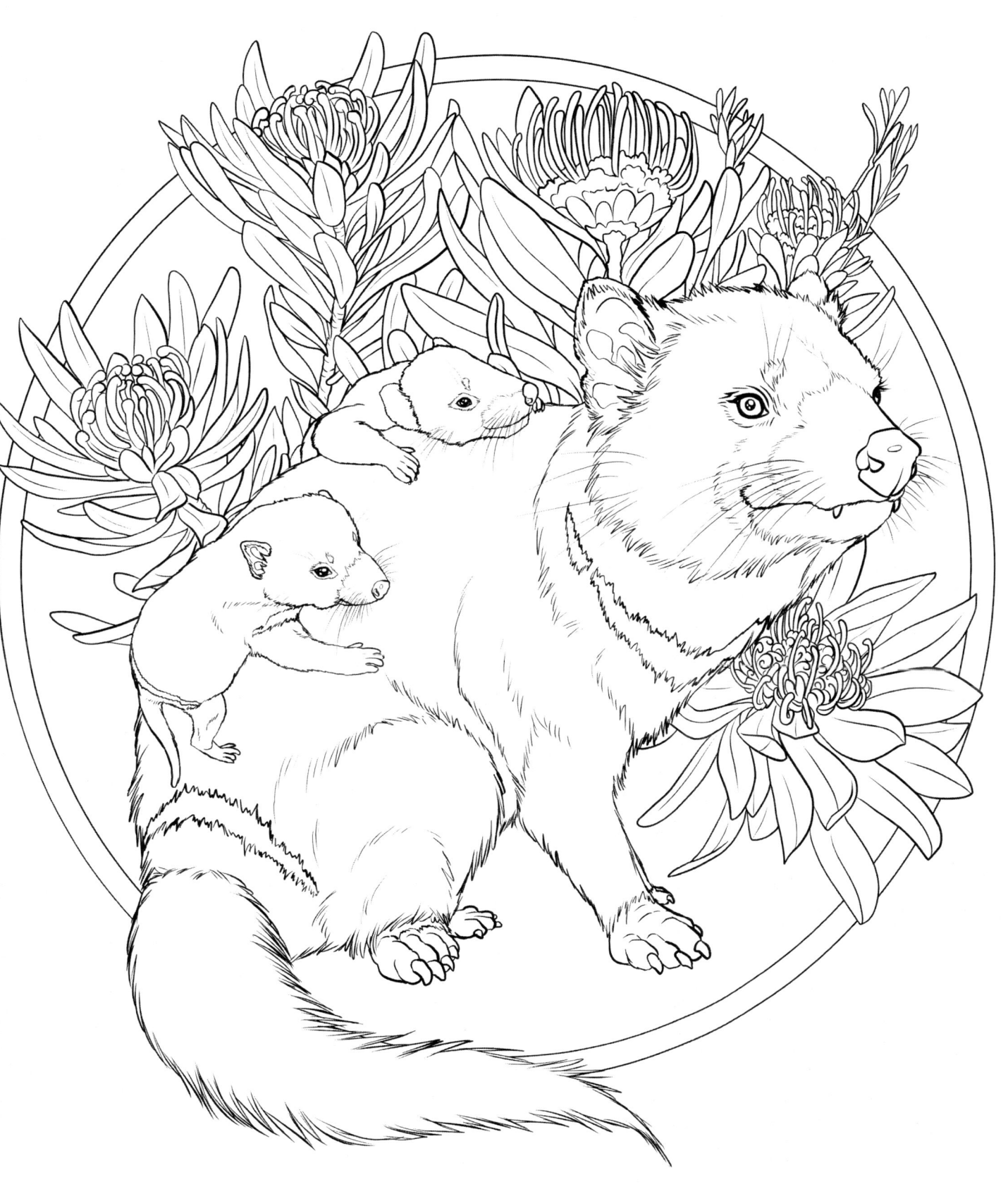

EMUS AND GYMEA LILY

The flightless emu is the world's second largest bird by height, growing up to two metres tall. Eggs and babies are cared for by the male. Gymea lilies have bright red flowers held high above their strappy green leaves on long spears.

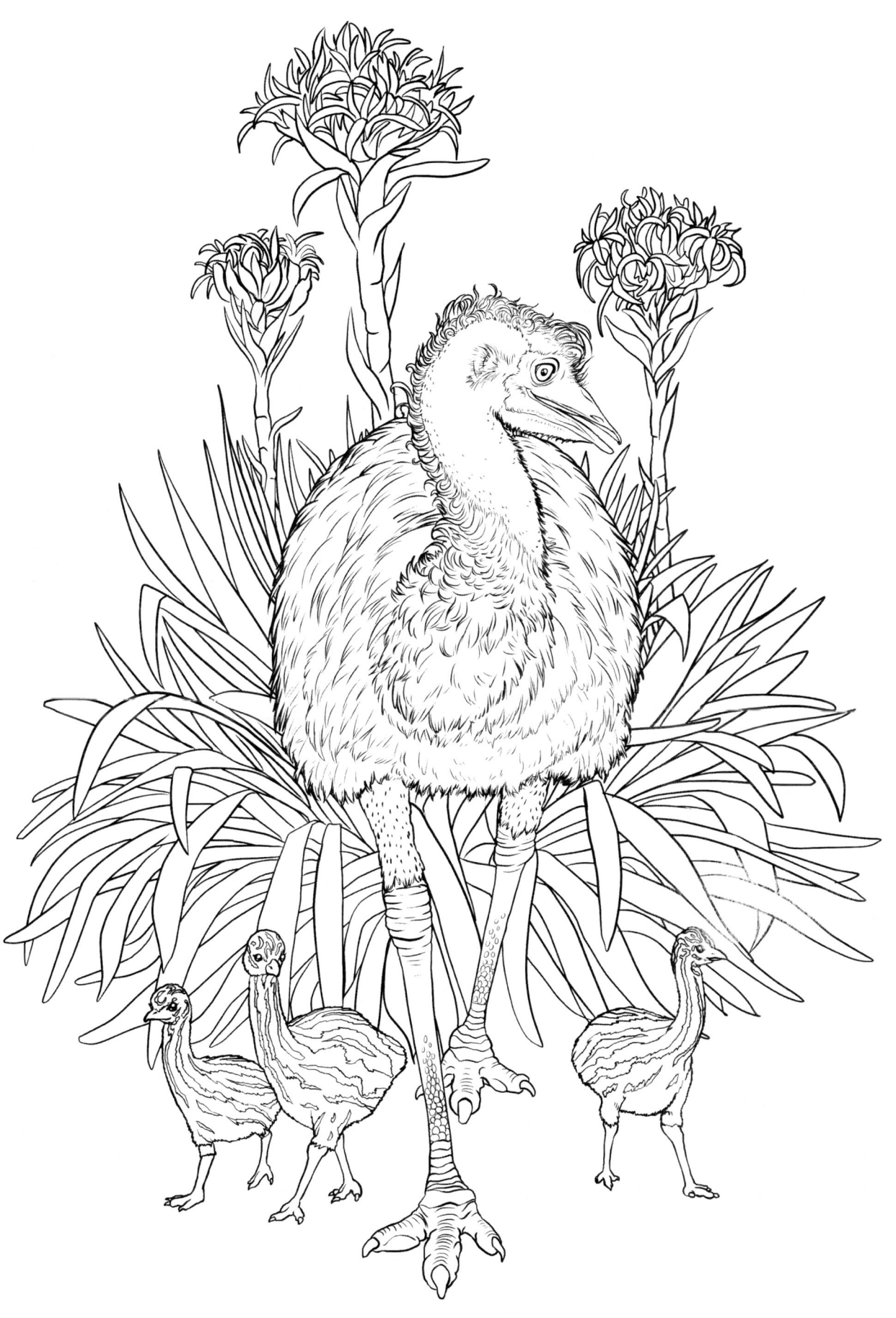

DINGOS AND MOUNTAIN DEVIL

Australia's wild dog, dingos are commonly sandy coloured but can also be black, black and tan, and white. They do not bark, but rather howl like wolves. The mountain devil is a red-flowering shrub that forms pointed seed follicles that resemble devil heads.

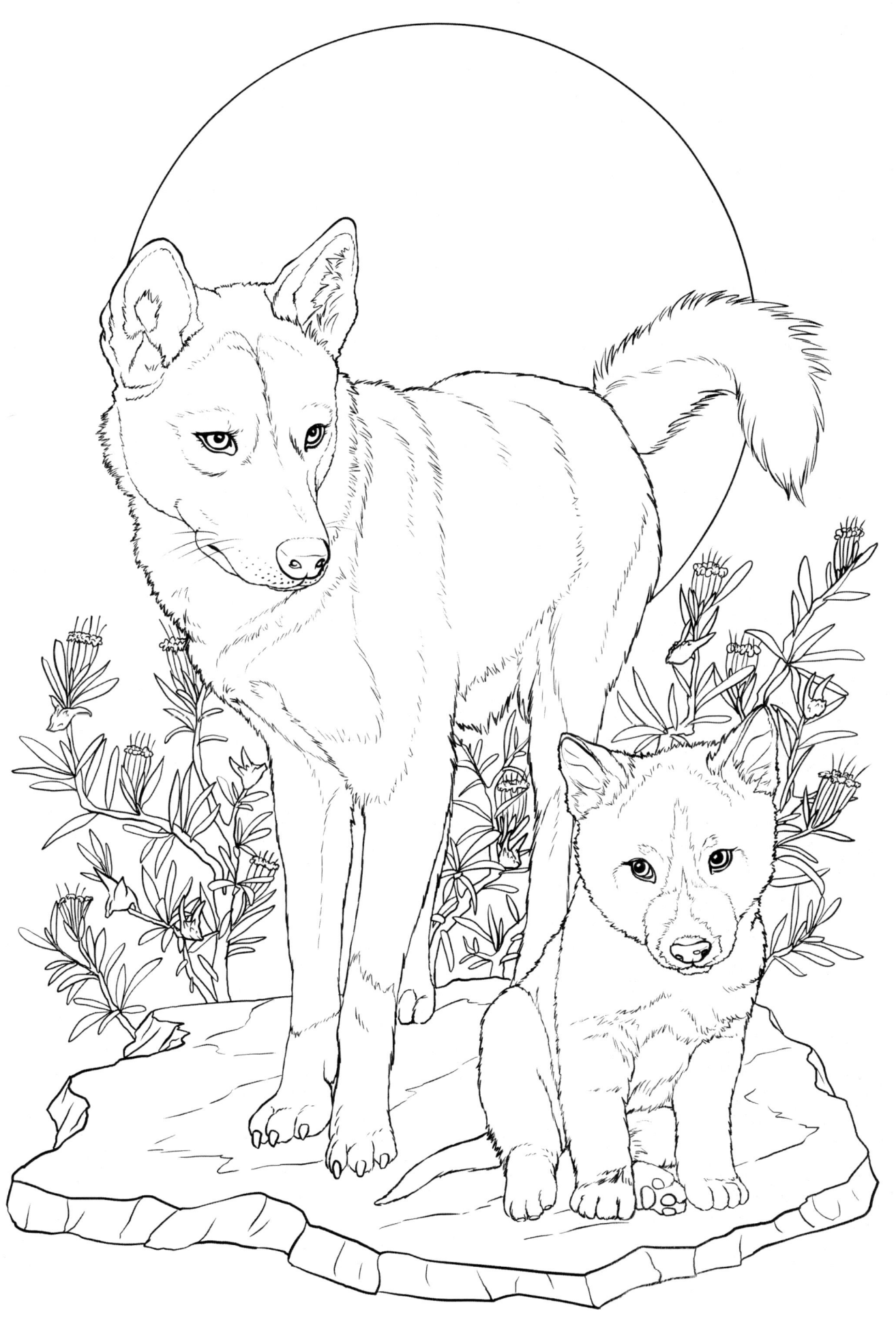

BLUE-WINGED KOOKABURRA AND BANKSIAS

Famous for its laugh, this kookaburra has a white head and chest, brown back and wings with bright blue highlights. There are over 170 species of banksias. Their iconic cylindrical shaped flower spikes come in a range of colours of a vibrant sunset.

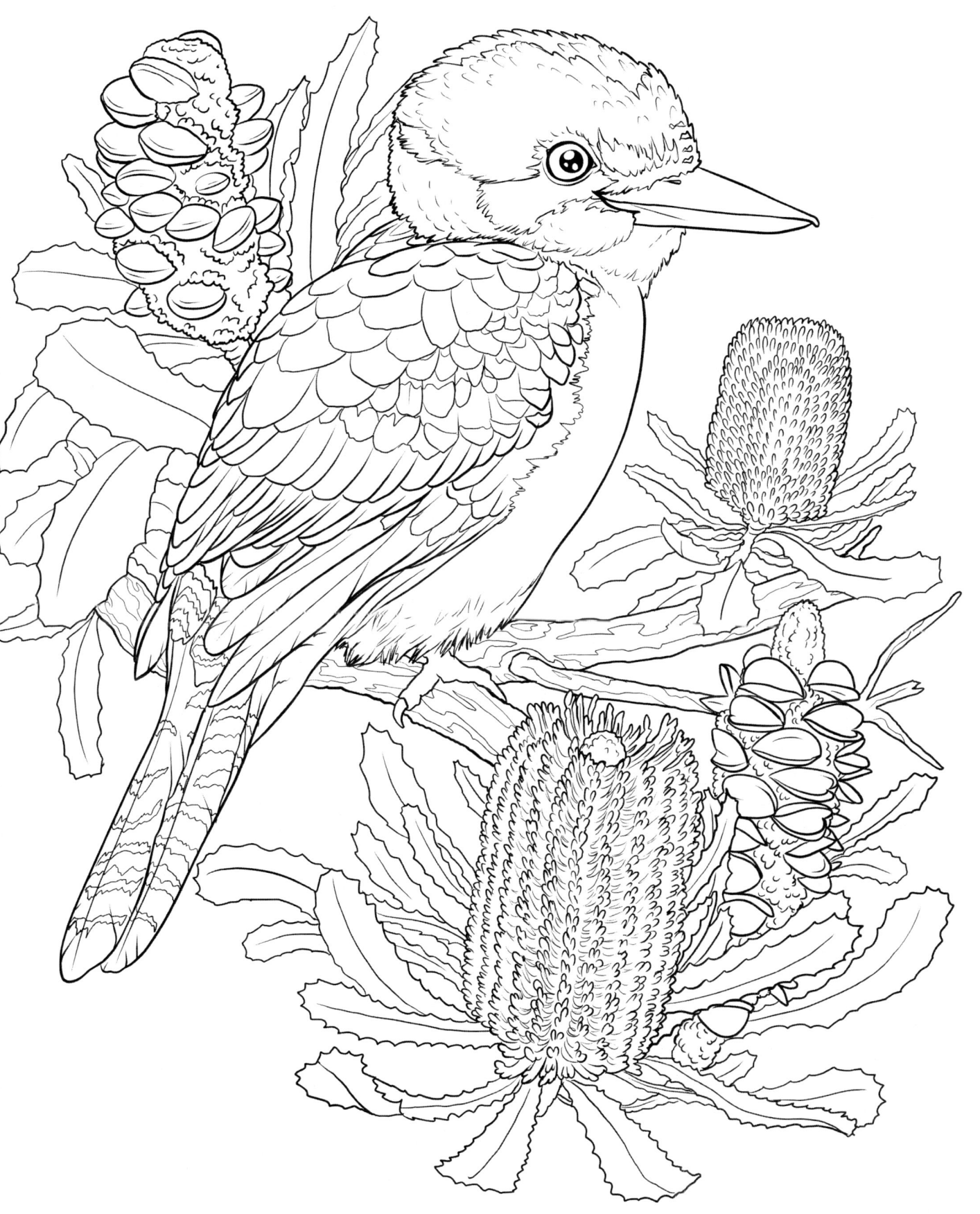

RAKALI WITH RAINBOW NARDOO

Australia's water rat, with rich brown fur and pale yellow-to-orange underside, the rakali recently became famous for being able to eat cane toads without being poisoned. Nardoo is a waterplant related to ferns, which grows in the form of a four-leafed clover. Its leaves range from pale green to rusty-red in tone.

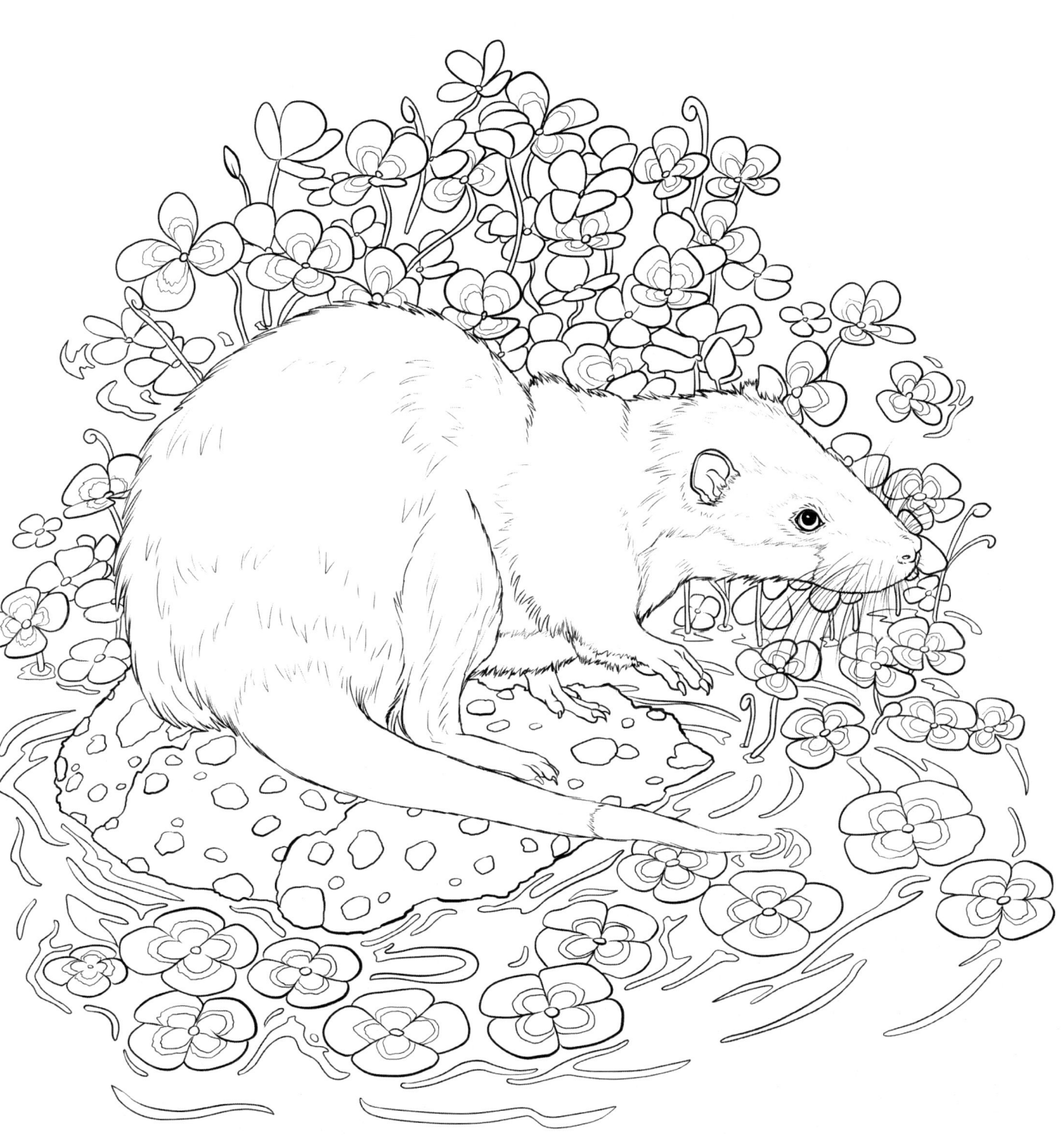

BROLGA WITH CUMBUNGI

Brolgas are famous for their courtship displays, involving elaborate dancing. This pale grey crane has a red head and stands almost human height. Cumbungi are strappy green water plants, most notable for their sausage-like seed head.

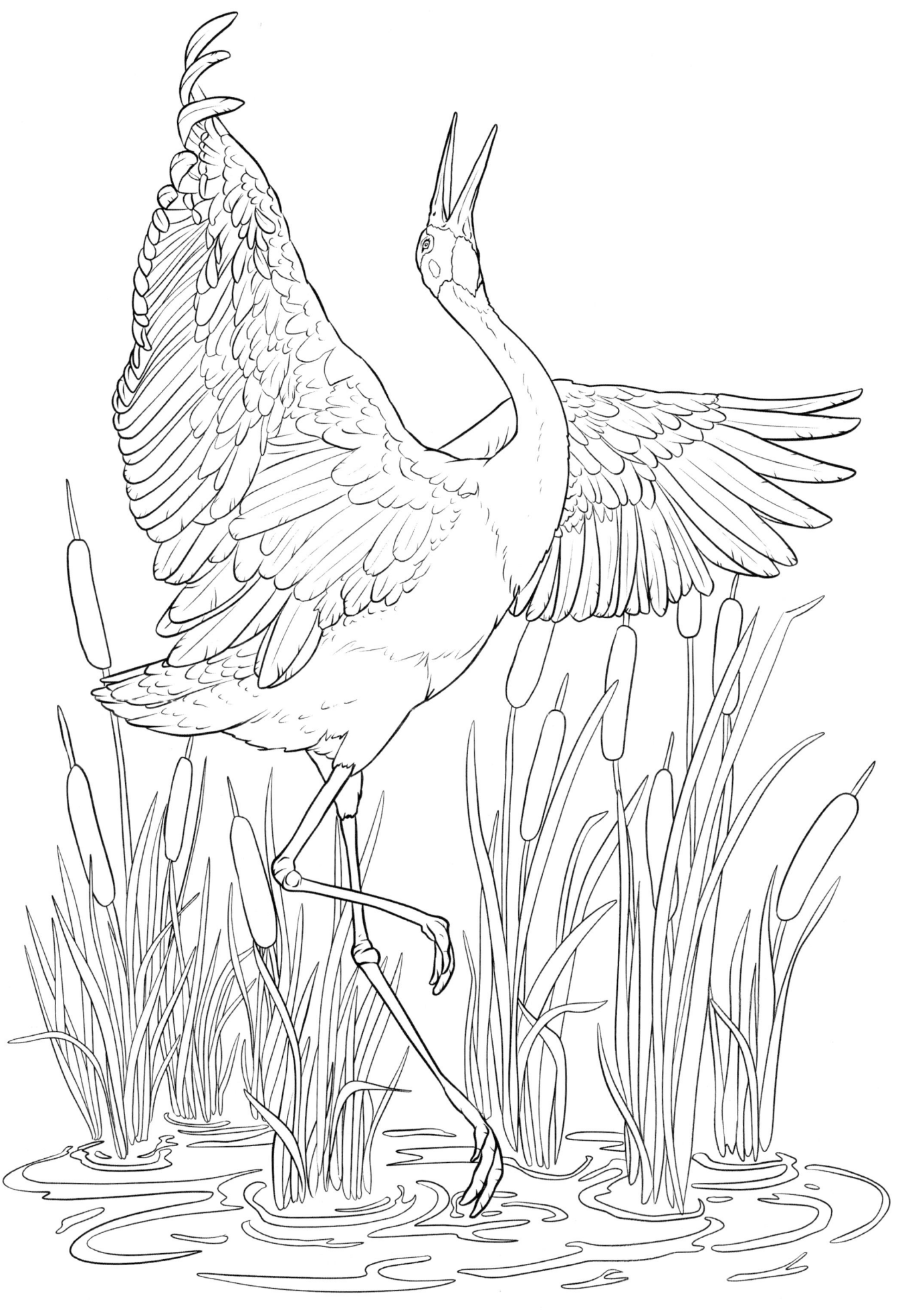

BILBIES AND FLANNEL FLOWERS

Silky, silvery grey bilbies are rabbit-sized and nocturnal. Flannel flowers take their name from the velvety soft feel, with pale green centres and white petals with green tips.

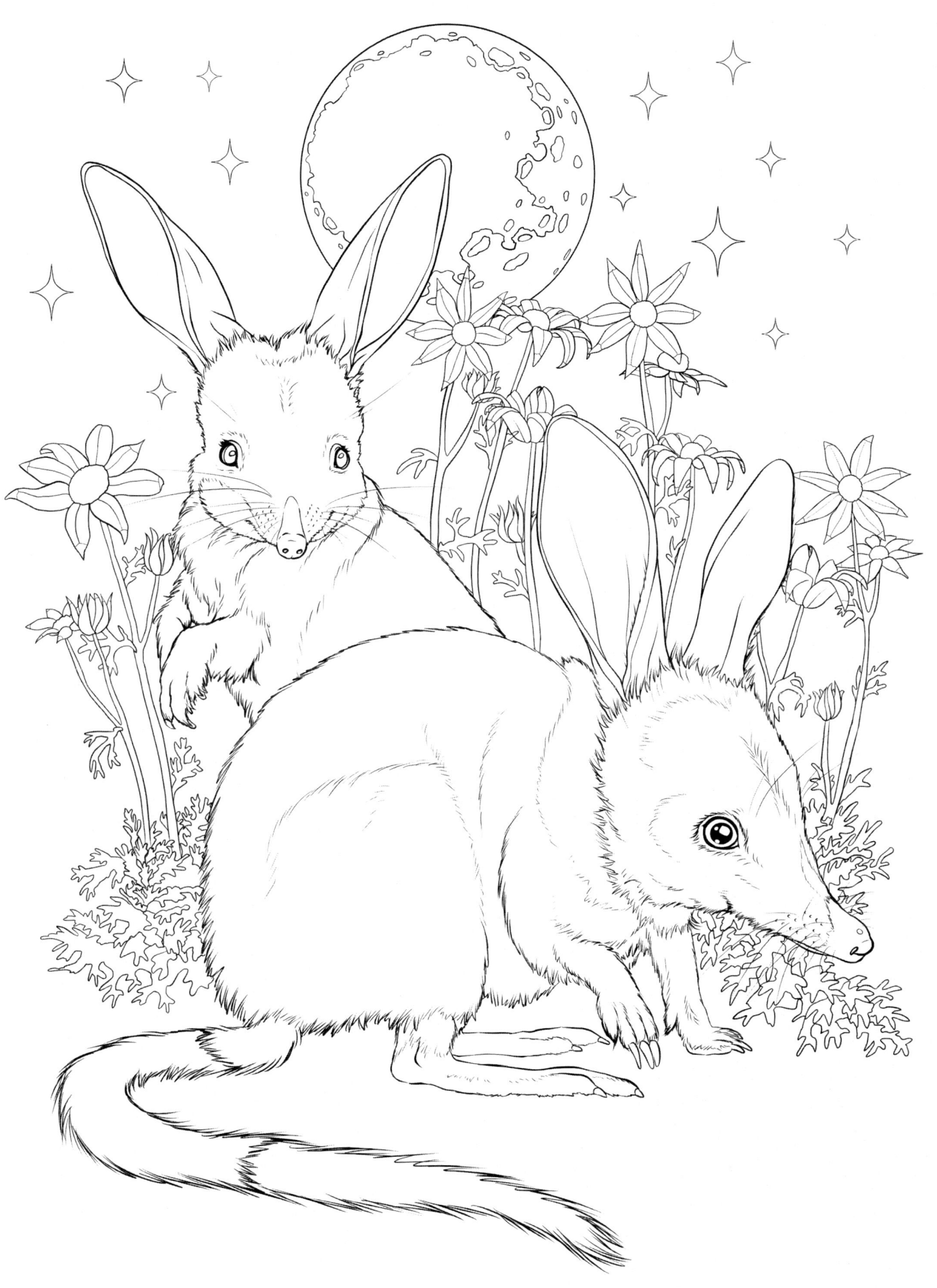

NUMBATS AND CHRISTMAS BELLS

Numbats are insectevorous, eating termites with their long tongues. They have no pouch, rather their babies cling onto the mothers belly. They have russet fur, darkening to black over their rump, with white stripes. Christmas bell flowers are bright red with vibrant yellow tips.

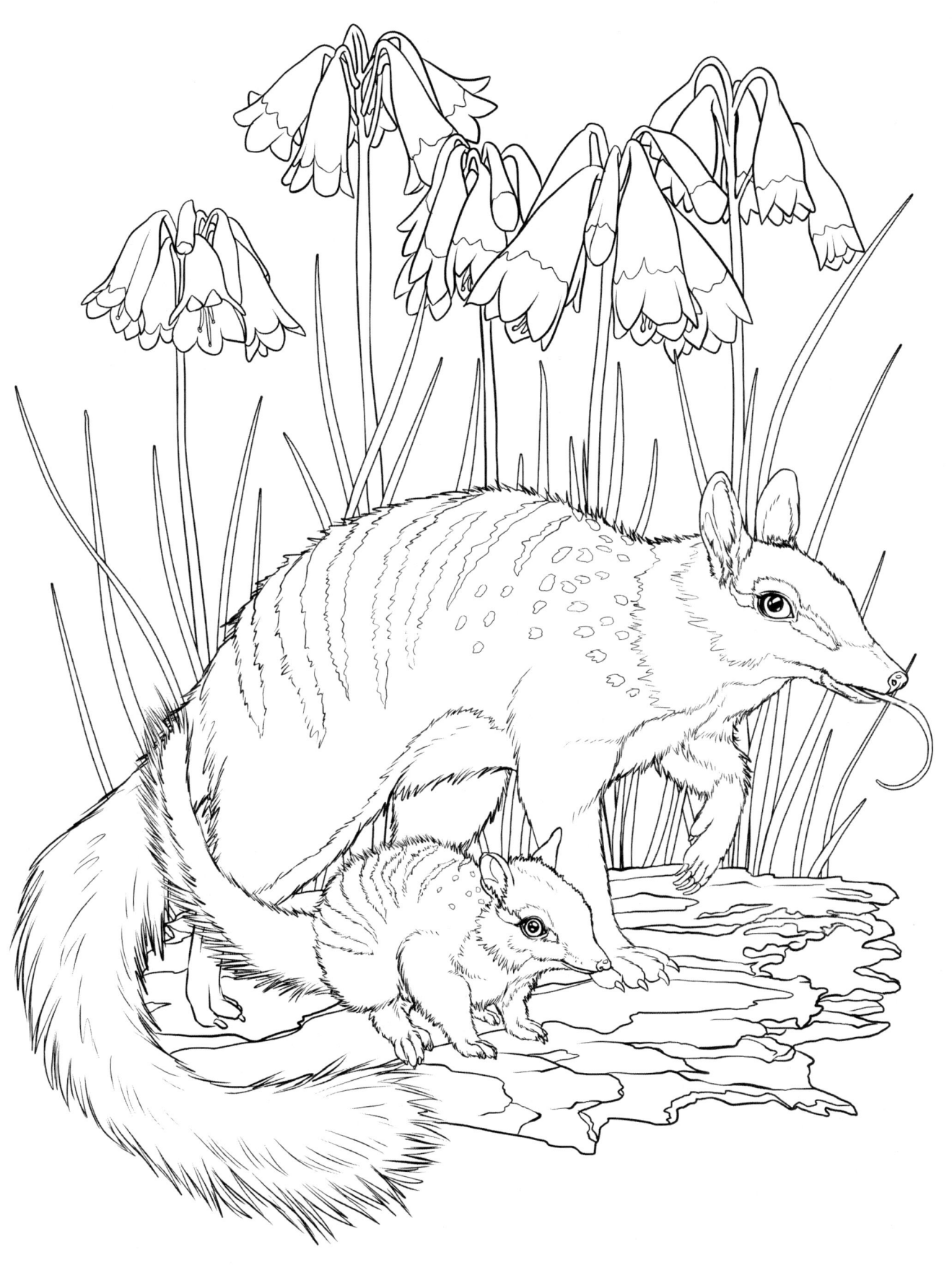

GOANNA WITH STURT'S DESERT PEA

Also known as the lace monitor, goannas can grow over two metres long. Their patterned scales in yellows and blacks provide camouflage, and they swallow their prey whole. Sturt's desert pea is most famously bright red with a black centre, but can also be pink and white.

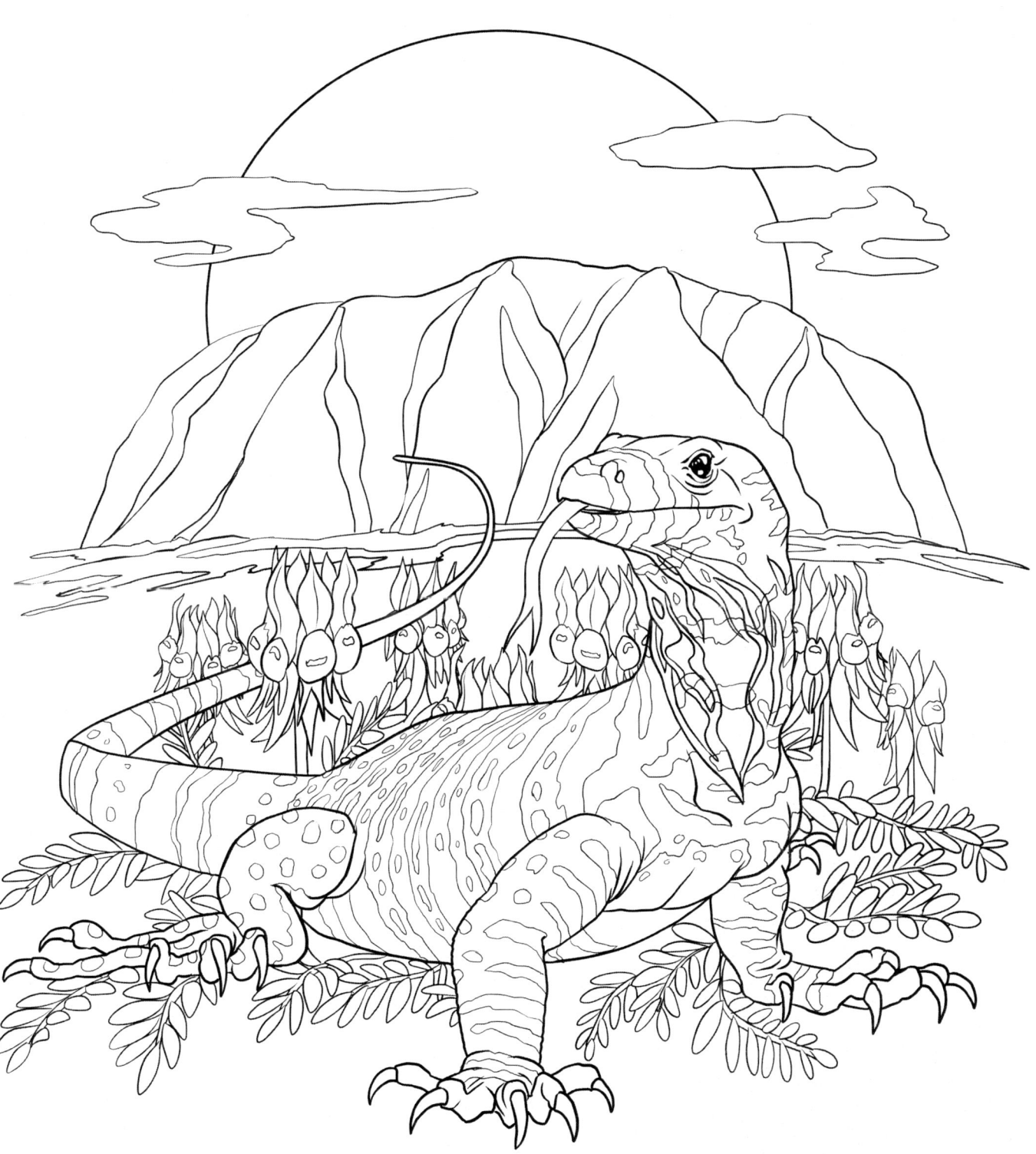

GREY-HEADED FLYING FOXES WITH LILLY PILLY

Flying foxes, or fruit bats, live in large communities. They have large black wings, rusty-red neck fur and grey heads. Lilly pillies grow multitudes of pink fruits, and often have pink and red tipped leaves.

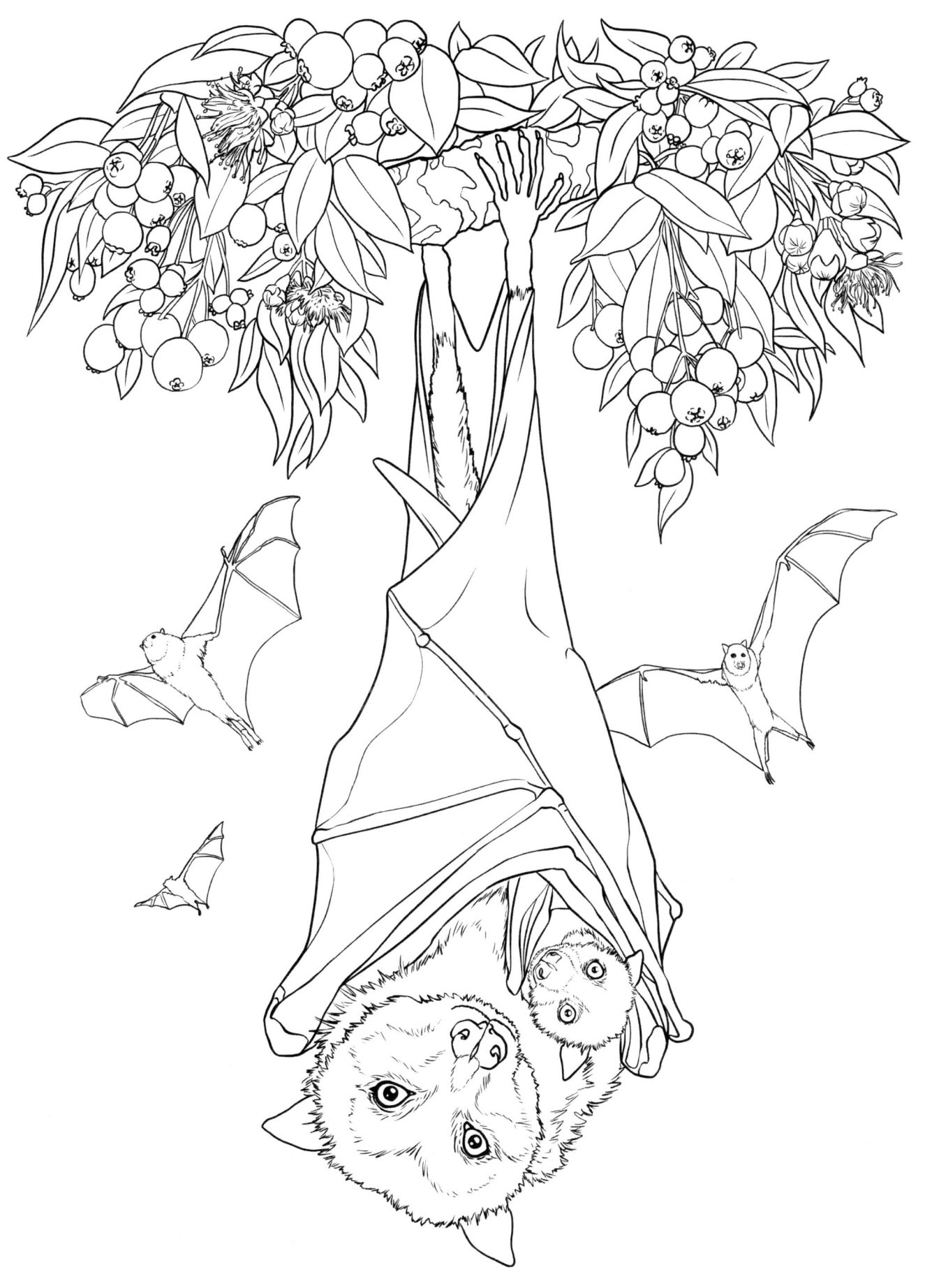

GOLDEN BELL FROG AND ALBANY PITCHER PLANTS

This green and gold coloured frog is one of Australia's largest, growing up to eleven centimetres long. The bright green and red jug-shaped traps of the Albany pitcher plant lure in insects which it eats.

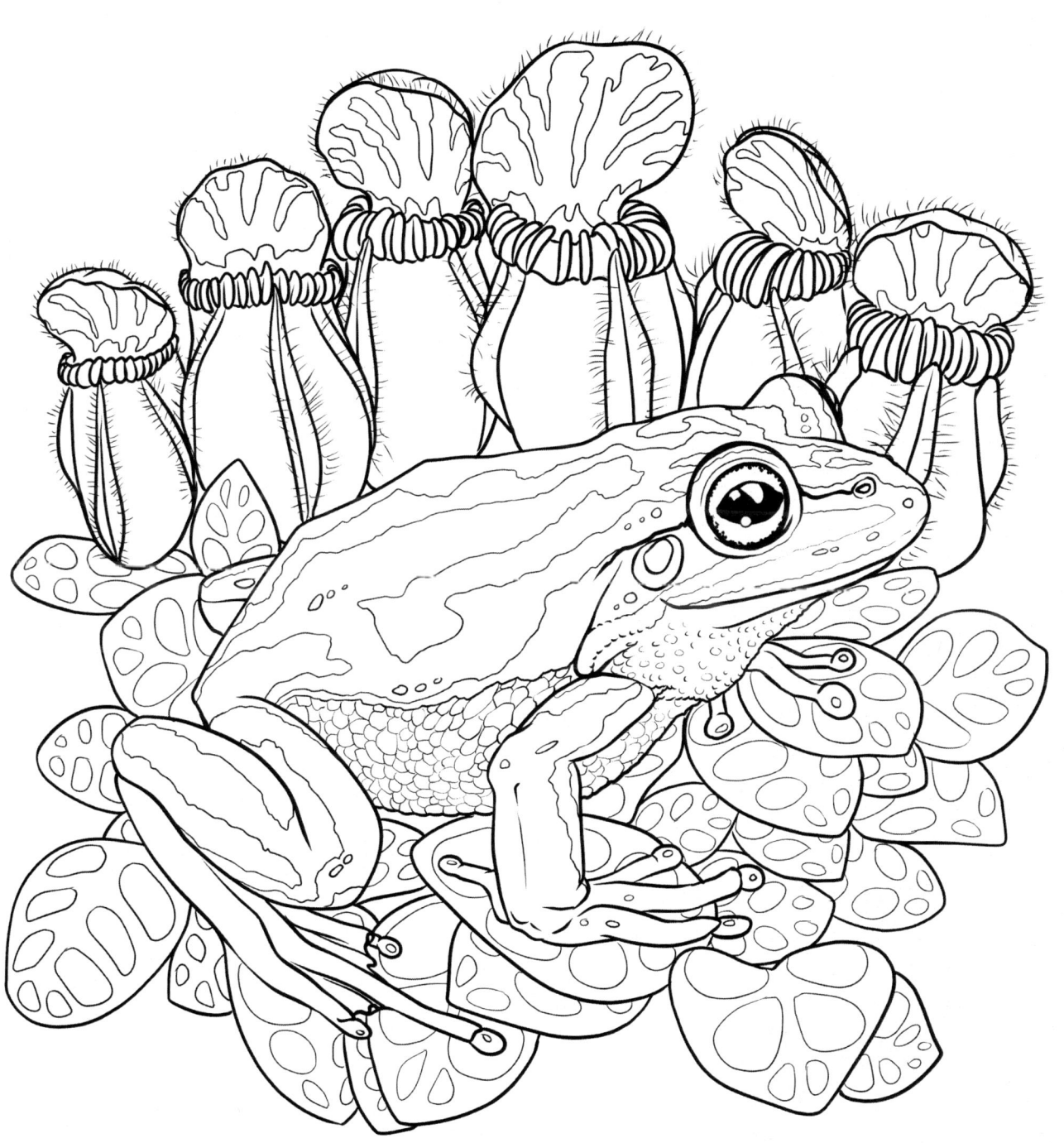

SUGAR GLIDER WITH LACEBARK KURRAJONG

Pale grey with cream belly and black stripes, the sugar glider is a tiny marsupial. It has the ability to glide using mebranes which stretch between its wrists and ankles. The lacebark kurrajong is a large tree with bright pink flowers.

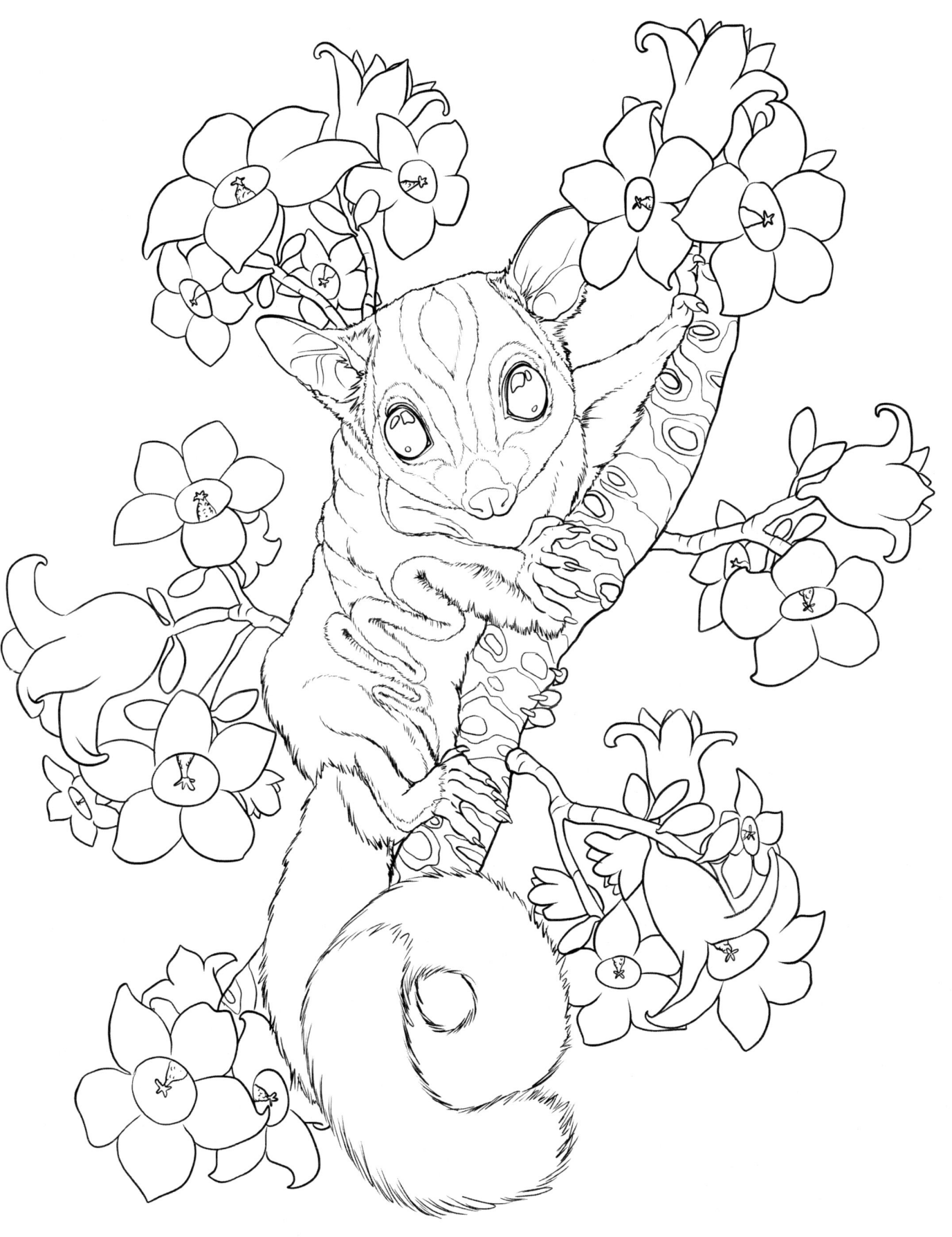

BEARDED DRAGON WITH BLUE DAMPIERA

These lizards appear in a range of stone and earth colours, from warm orange to charcoal grey, and can grow up to 55 centimetres in length. They will enlarge their spikey throats when threatened.
The blue dampiera is a small wildflower with striking blue blossoms.

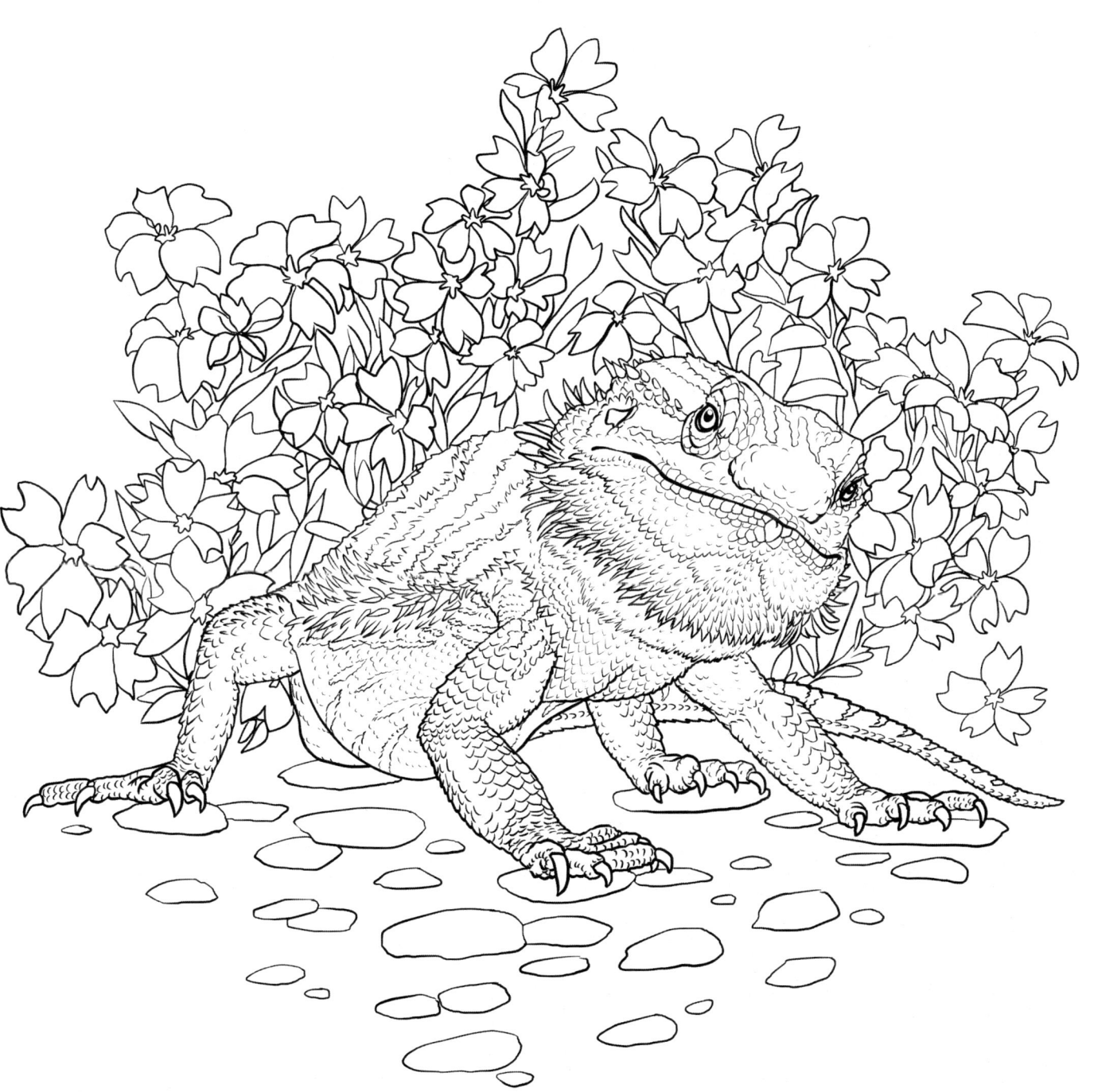

CORROBOREE FROGS AND SUNDEWS

These boldly patterned black and yellow frogs are small enough to fit on the tip of your finger. Sundew's bright green and red leaves are covered in tiny hairs with sticky mucilage, designed to trap insects on which this plant feeds.

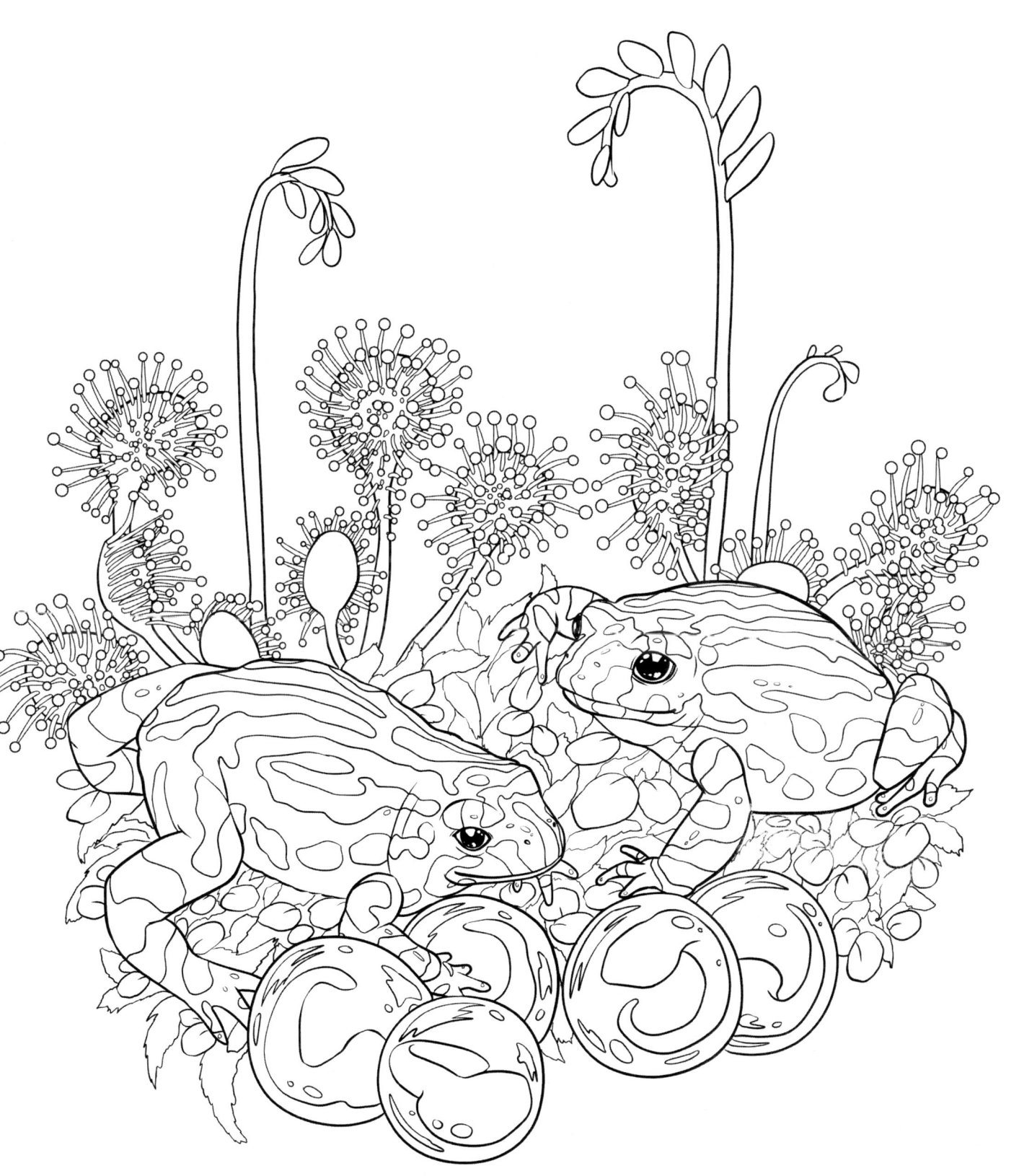

COLORING BOOKS

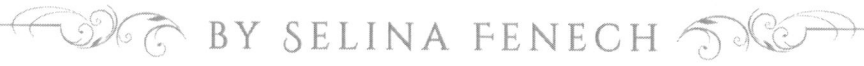

BY SELINA FENECH

So much more magic to color!

More than 25 colouring titles available,
from standard books, to pocket sized editions,
grayscale editions, and coloring journals.

Try out some mini samples
on the following pages.

Discover more at www.selinafenech.com

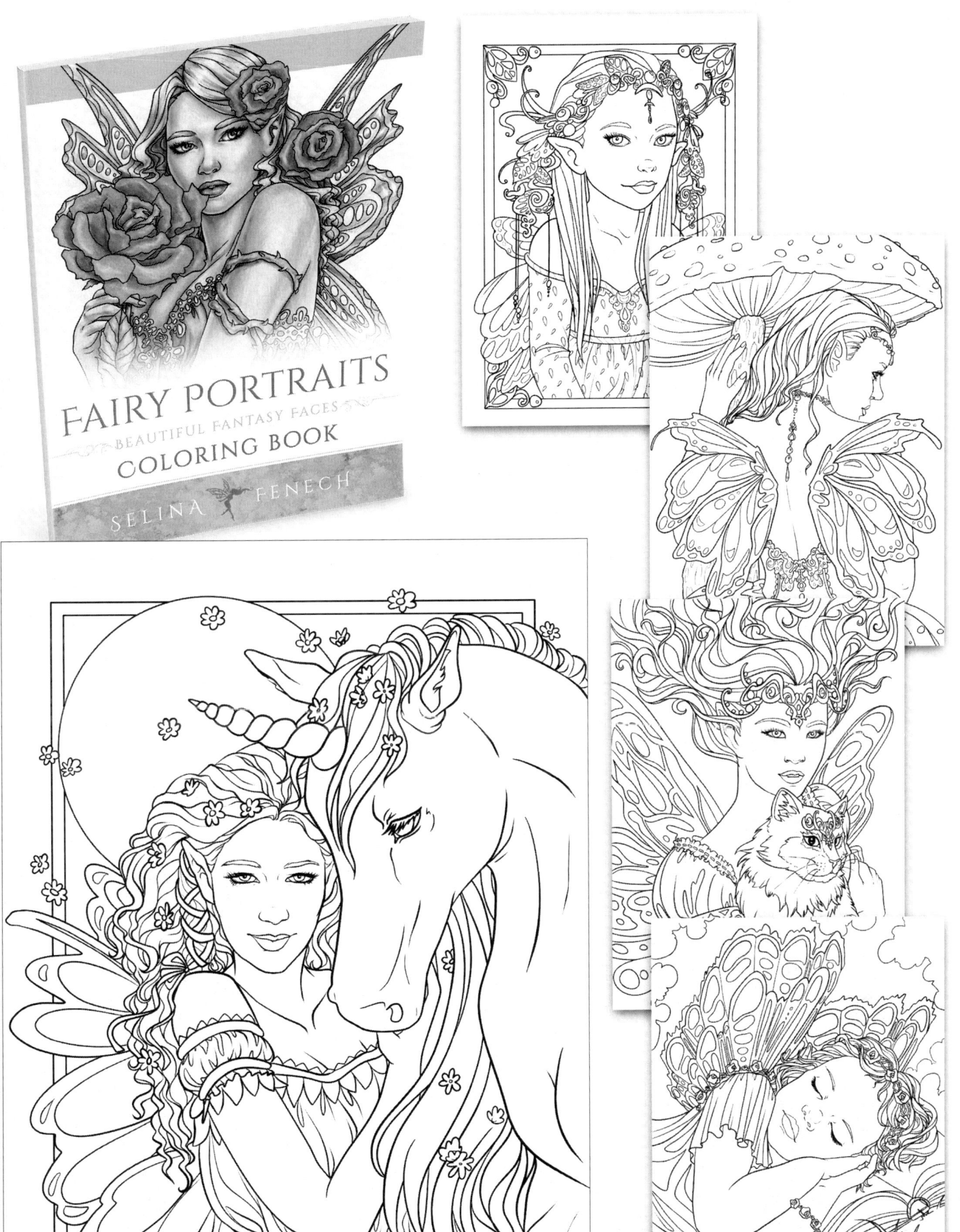

GRAYSCALE COLORING
EDITIONS

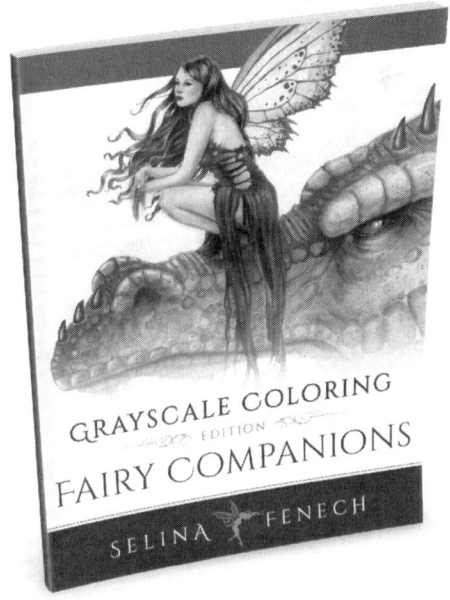
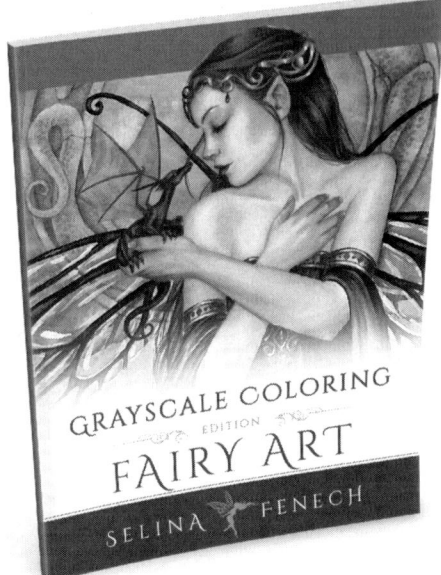
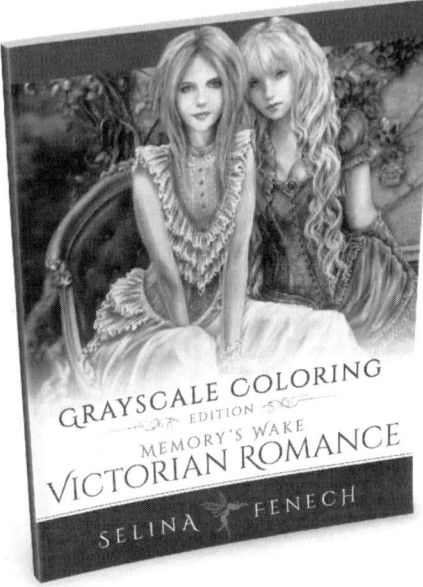
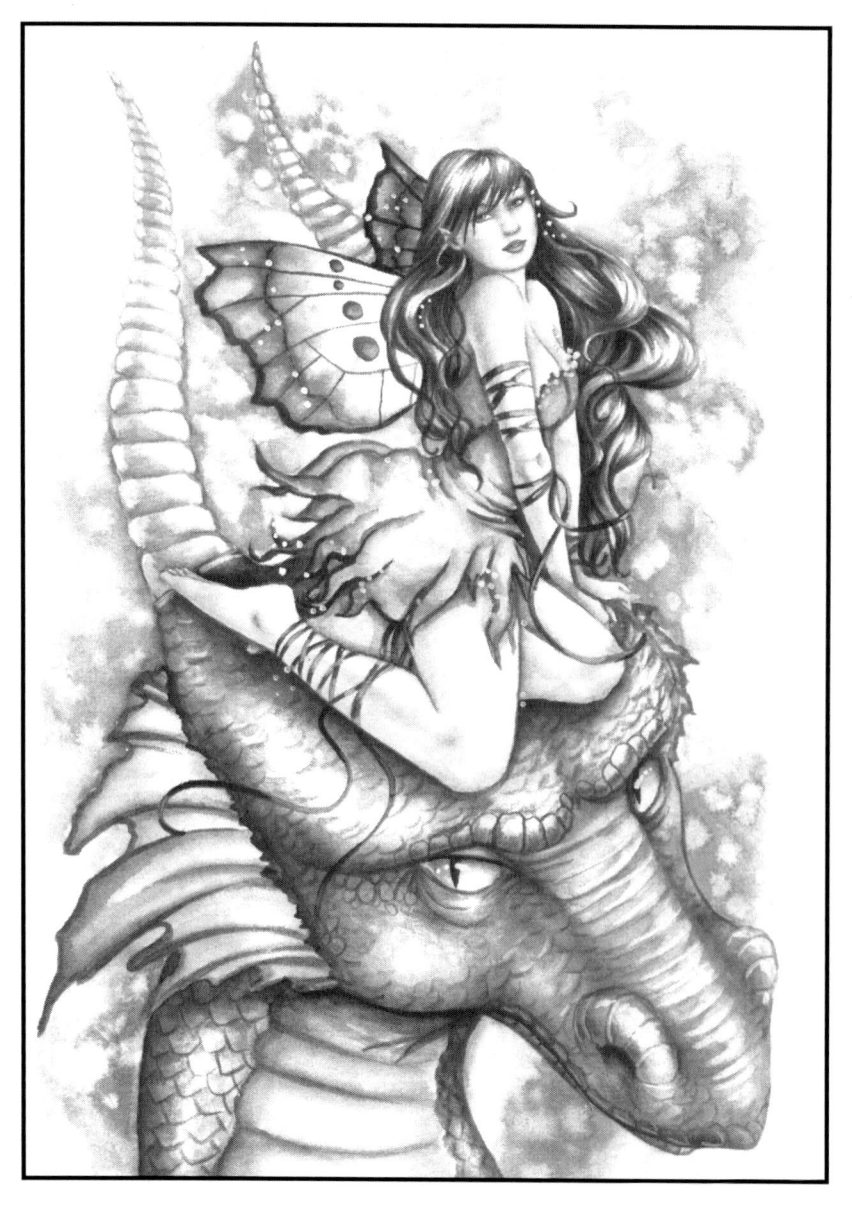
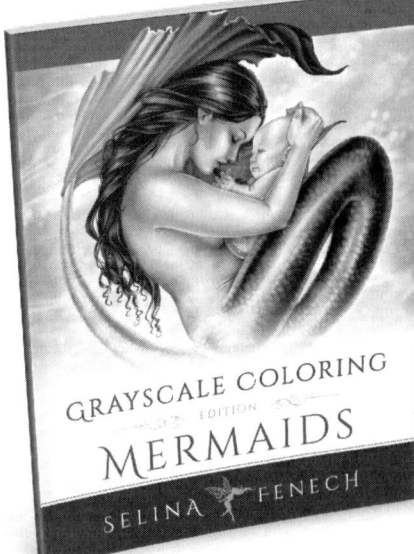
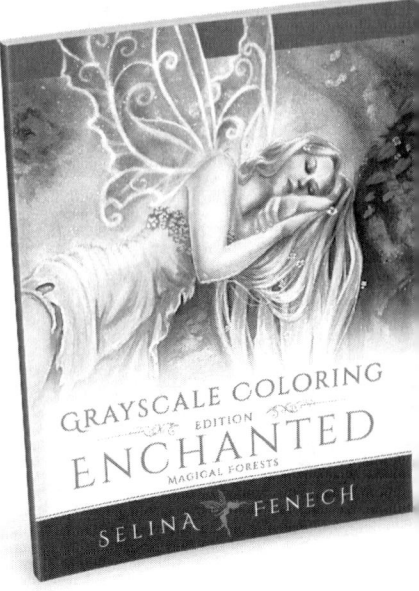

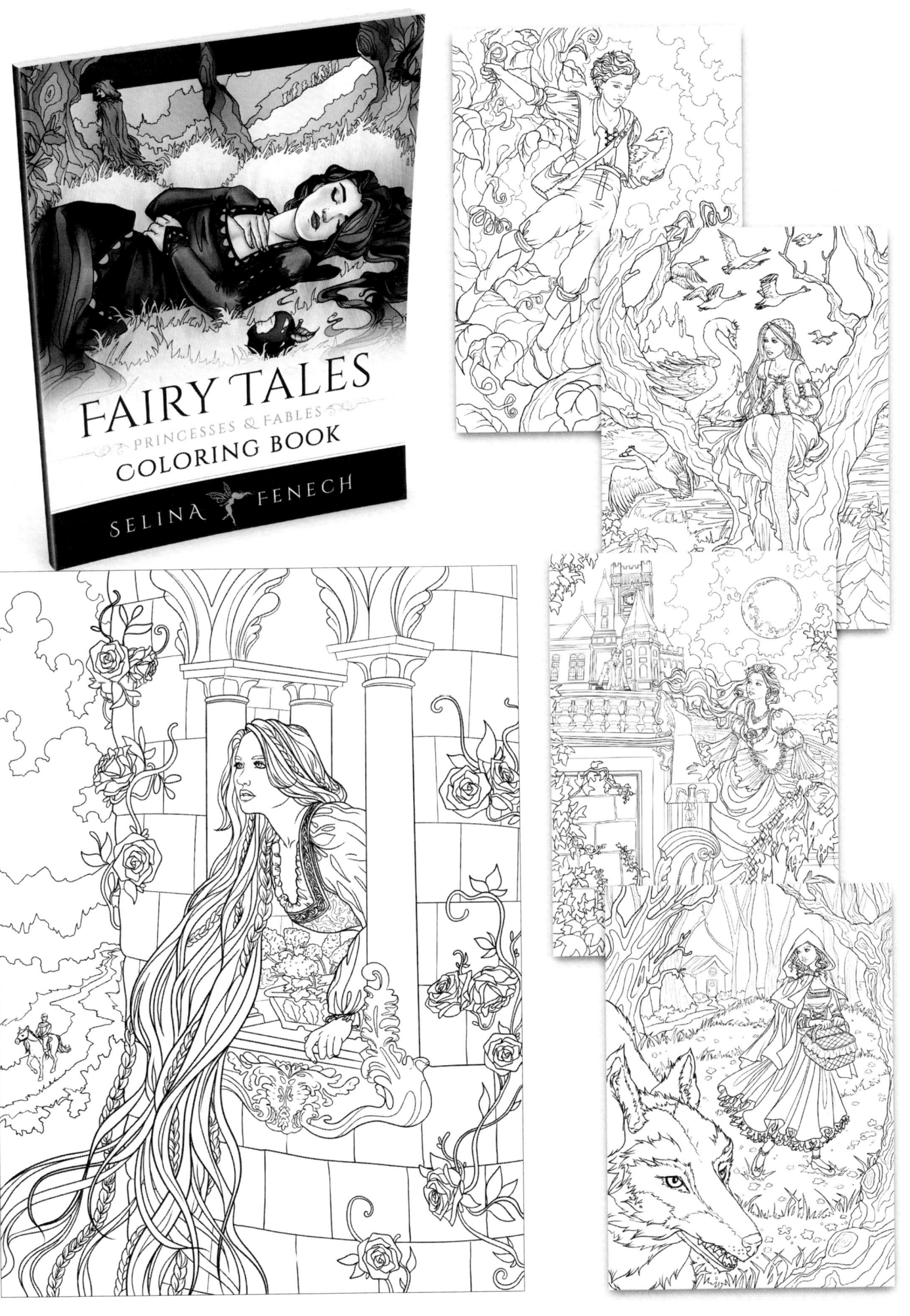

About the Artist

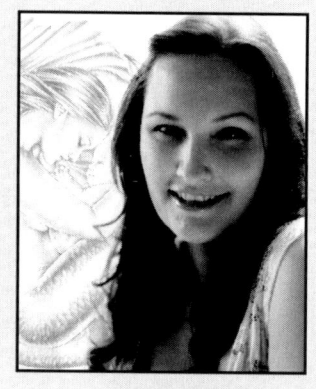

As a lover of all things fantasy, Selina has made a living as an artist since she was 23 years old selling her magical creations. Her works range from oil paintings to oracle decks, dolls to digital scrapbooking, plus Young Adult novels, jewelry, and coloring books.

Born in 1981 to Australian and Maltese parents, Selina lives in Australia with her husband, daughter, and growing urban farm menagerie.

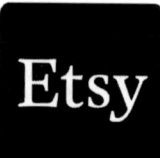

Download printable coloring pages from all of Selina's coloring books at
www.etsy.com/shop/printablefantasy

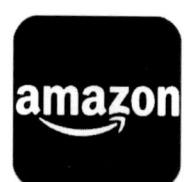

See all of Selina's bestselling coloring books, journals, art books and more at
amazon.com/author/selina

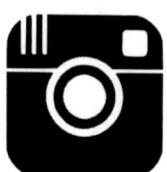

Sneak a peek into Selina's studio and see what she's working on now at
instagram.com/selinafenech/

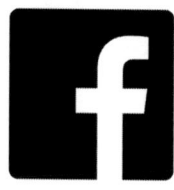

Get social with Selina and see how others are coloring her work in her coloring group at **bit.ly/colorselina**

Using This Book

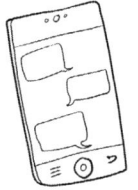

Turn off and move away from distractions. Relax into the peaceful process of coloring and enjoy the magic of these fantasy images.

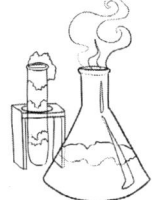

Experiment! There is no right or wrong way to color, and with two of each image, there's no pressure.

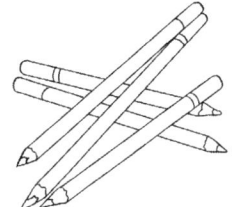

This book works best with color pencils or markers. Wet mediums should be used sparingly. Slip a piece of card behind the image you're working on in case the markers bleed through.

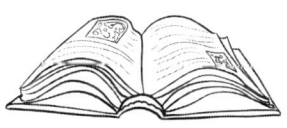

Don't be scared to dismantle this book. Cut finished pages out to frame, or split the book in half where the second set of images start so you and a loved one can color together.

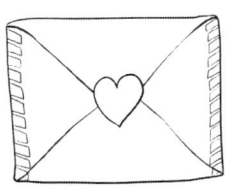

Never run out of fantasy coloring pages by signing up to Selina's newsletter. Get free downloadable pages and updates on new books at -
selinafenech.com/free-coloring-sampler/

Share Your Work

 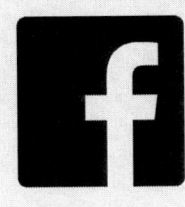

Share on Instagram with #colorselina
to be included in Selina's coloring gallery,
and visit the gallery for inspiration.

selinafenech.com/coloringgallery

Made in United States
North Haven, CT
09 September 2024

57206757R00061